RELATIONSHIPS & BELONGING

WHY STUDENTS STRUGGLE IN ISOLATION BUT THRIVE IN CONNECTION

Funding to help underwrite the development of
the *15-Minute Focus* series has been generously provided by:

The Sarah T. Butler Children's Center at the Pastoral Institute of Columbus, Georgia is dedicated to the mental health and well-being of children ages 1-18. This center provides comprehensive services that span psychological testing, intervention, therapy groups, and counseling. In all our activities we seek to inspire growth through faith, hope, and love.

Duplication and Copyright

NCYI titles may be purchased in bulk at special discounts for educational, business, fundraising, or promotional use. For more information, please email sales@ncyi.org.

NATIONAL CENTER for YOUTH ISSUES

P.O. Box 22185
Chattanooga, TN 37422-2185
423.899.5714 • 866.318.6294
fax: 423.899.4547 • www.ncyi.org

Print: 9781965066393
eBook: 9781965066430

The Library of Congress Control Number has been applied for and can be obtained with the Library of Congress.

© 2026 National Center for Youth Issues, Chattanooga, TN
All rights reserved.
Written by: Amy Baltimore
Published by National Center for Youth Issues
Printed in the U.S.A. • May 2026

Contents

**See page 139 for information about
Downloadable Resources and Templates**

See page 139 for information about Downloadable Resources and Templates

Introduction

Living in Eastern Europe after the fall of Communism, I saw firsthand the intensely damaging effects of isolation on a child's development. Babies in state-run orphanages who turned their heads away instead of responding to a smile, children who listlessly drew circles in the dirt instead of engaging in play, and teenagers whose hardened eyes and aloof stance warned against any interaction. At the time, I wondered if these behaviors were confined only to that setting.

Fast-forward to today and stand in the doorway of a modern classroom. The scene can be deceptively lively and engaging. Students comment to each other as they unpack backpacks, peers exchange inside jokes, and a few gather around a laptop to watch a short video, while others scribble last-minute homework.

The room hums with movement and noise; yet inside the crowd are students who feel deeply alone and isolated. They blend in, not by choice but out of habit. They move through the day with little connection to what's going on around them, often unnoticed.

This is one of the paradoxes within the modern school experience: **high visibility/low connectedness.**

Students may be surrounded by people at every moment of the day yet lack even a single relationship that feels emotionally safe or meaningful. And because their disconnection is often quiet, polite, or masked by performance, it can be overlooked even by caring, attentive educators.

Isolation is not merely a social issue. It is a **neurological state** that erodes learning readiness, executive function, and emotional regulation. Most importantly, it is preventable when adults know what to look for.

The encouraging reality is this: *isolation is not inevitable*. When adults understand how belonging operates beneath the surface, they can create environments where students' nervous systems register safety often enough to support connection, growth, and learning.

The pages ahead draw on the language of neuroscience, safety, and belonging. The terms below are placed here, rather than at the back of the book, because understanding them early makes everything that follows more recognizable.

Glossary of Terms

Amygdala

A small structure in the brain that detects threats and activates the body's stress response. Often described as the brain's "alarm system," it becomes more reactive when a person feels unsafe or disconnected.

Example: A student snaps or shuts down quickly after a minor correction because their brain has registered the interaction as a threat.

Co-Regulation

The process by which one person helps another regulate their emotional or physiological state through calm presence, tone, and interaction. In schools, adults often serve as co-regulators for students.

Example: A teacher kneels beside a frustrated student, speaks softly, and helps them slow their breathing before returning to the task.

Cortisol

A stress hormone that is released when the brain perceives danger. While helpful in short bursts, prolonged elevation can impair memory, focus, and learning.

Example: A student experiencing ongoing stress at home struggles to concentrate or retain new information during lessons.

Dopamine

A neurotransmitter associated with motivation, reward, and engagement. It increases when individuals experience success, connection, or positive anticipation.

Example: A student becomes more engaged and eager to participate after receiving specific, positive feedback on their effort.

Dorsal Vagal State

A nervous system state associated with shutdown, withdrawal, and disconnection. This response often occurs after prolonged stress or when a person feels overwhelmed or unsafe.

Example: A student puts their head down, avoids interaction, and appears disengaged after repeated academic frustration.

Emotional Regulation

The ability to manage and respond to emotional experiences in a balanced and adaptive way. Strong emotional regulation supports learning, relationships, and decision-making.

Example: A student feels frustrated during a task but uses a strategy, such as deep breathing or asking for help, rather than giving up.

Executive Function

A set of mental skills—including working memory, flexible thinking, and self-control—that enable goal-directed behavior, problem-solving, and learning.

Example: A student follows multi-step directions, manages their time, and adjusts their approach when a strategy isn't working.

Hypervigilance

A heightened state of alertness in which the brain continuously scans for potential threats. This state is common in individuals experiencing chronic stress or instability.

Example: A student is easily startled by classroom noises and constantly watches others rather than focusing on their work.

Neural Pathways

Connections between neurons in the brain that are strengthened through repeated experiences. These pathways shape behavior, habits, and emotional responses over time.

Example: A classroom routine practiced daily becomes automatic, helping students transition smoothly without reminders.

Neural Safety Signals

Brief verbal and nonverbal cues—such as tone of voice, eye contact, or acknowledgment—that communicate safety to the brain and help shift it out of a threat response.

Example: Greeting students by name at the door and making eye contact show students they are seen, valued, and safe.

Neuroception

The brain's automatic and unconscious process of detecting whether situations or people are safe, dangerous, or life-threatening, without deliberate thought.

Example: A student relaxes in one classroom but feels tense in another without being able to explain why.

Nervous System

The body's communication network that regulates thoughts, emotions, and physical responses. It continuously interprets environmental cues to determine safety or threat.

Example: A calm, predictable classroom helps students' nervous systems stay regulated and ready to learn.

Oxytocin

A hormone associated with bonding, trust, and social connection. It is released during positive interactions and supports feelings of safety and belonging.

Example: A student feels more connected and willing to participate after a positive interaction with a trusted teacher.

Parasympathetic Nervous System

The branch of the nervous system responsible for calming the body. It slows heart rate, supports digestion, and helps restore balance and regulation.

Example: After a calming routine or quiet moment, a student is able to refocus and engage in learning.

Polyvagal Theory

A framework developed by Dr. Stephen Porges that explains how the nervous system responds to safety and threat through different pathways, influencing social engagement, fight-or-flight, or shutdown responses.

Example: A teacher recognizes when a student is in a state of fight-or-flight and responds with calming strategies rather than punishment.

Prefrontal Cortex (PFC)

The part of the brain responsible for higher-order thinking, including decision-making, planning, impulse control, and empathy. It functions best when a person feels safe and regulated.

Example: A student is able to solve problems and think critically after settling down from an emotional upset.

Ventral Vagal State

A nervous system state associated with safety, connection, and social engagement. In this state, individuals are calm, open, and ready to learn.

Example: Students collaborate, ask questions, and take academic risks in a classroom where they feel safe and connected.

Isolation, belonging, safety, connection—these are not abstract ideals. They are biological realities that shape how students show up every day. This book invites you to look again at the students in your care, not only at what they are doing, but also at what their nervous systems may be experiencing. You do not have to overhaul your classroom or try to fix every moment of disconnection—small, consistent signals of safety matter. As you move through these pages, identify where belonging practices are already present in your school and consider where even one intentional shift could make a difference.

The chapters ahead translate that science into what you can see, do, and change. We begin where it all starts: *learning to recognize disconnection before it becomes damage.*

Diagnosing Disconnection

The Temporal Dimension of Belonging

Neuroscience teaches us that humans are wired to seek social safety and belonging. When environments are inconsistent or feel unwelcoming, the brain shifts into a defensive mode. Early experiences of exclusion or isolation can become embedded in neural pathways, shaping how students approach relationships, healthy risk-taking, and learning. Over time, these memories of being overlooked or excluded may resurface, causing students to protect themselves rather than lean into connection and engagement.

However, when students consistently encounter welcoming environments where they are seen, heard, and valued, their brains begin to expect that sense of safety and social reward. Over time, they become more willing to participate, ask questions, and stay engaged, even when learning feels challenging.

Dr. Stephen Porges' *Polyvagal Theory* helps explain this. When students perceive safety, their *ventral vagal system* engages, supporting social engagement, curiosity, and learning. When repeated experiences convey unpredictability or exclusion, the *dorsal vagal system* activates, leading to withdrawal, disengagement, or even learned helplessness. Sustaining a culture of belonging, therefore,

Polyvagal Theory

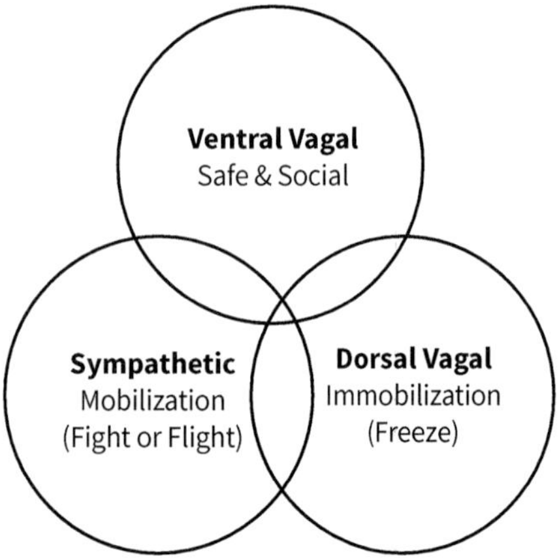

is not just about being nice; it is about consistently engaging the neural mechanisms that enable students to approach rather than avoid social and academic challenges.

Belonging is not simply about hanging a welcome banner or amping up the school's branding. It is about consistently engaging the neural mechanisms that allow students to approach rather than avoid social and academic challenges. The encouraging reality is this: *the effects of chronic isolation are not inevitable*. When adults understand how belonging operates beneath the surface, they can create environments in which students' nervous systems register safety often enough to support connection, growth, and learning.

The remainder of this initial chapter lays the foundation for everything that follows. Before we can transform school culture, intervene effectively, or implement belonging-focused practices, we must develop the ability to **diagnose disconnection,** which is to see the invisible patterns that tell us a student's nervous system is struggling. This requires a shift in mindset, deeper attunement to subtle cues, and an understanding of the difference between *healthy solitude* and *harmful isolation.*

Healthy Solitude vs. Harmful Isolation

Children and adolescents need moments of solitude. Quiet time can help students:

- regulate their thoughts
- decompress from overstimulation
- exercise creativity
- build independence

Healthy solitude is *voluntary*. It restores a student's nervous system. Isolation, however, is *involuntary*. It is the chronic experience of being on the outside of meaningful relationships, physically present but emotionally disconnected. Unlike healthy solitude, isolation **activates the body's threat response**.

Why Adults Confuse the Two

In schools, quiet or independent students are often praised:

- *"She's so mature—she just keeps to herself."*
- *"He doesn't need help; he's self-reliant."*
- *"They're low maintenance."*

But in many cases, these students are not self-reliant; they are **self-protective**. Their nervous systems have learned that staying small, silent, or unnoticed is safer than risking vulnerability.

This is especially true for students with:

- histories of school mobility
- unstable peer groups
- social anxiety
- cultural barriers
- chronic academic stress
- experiences of being excluded before

Isolation doesn't look the same across developmental stages.

Developmental Differences in How Isolation Shows Up		
Elementary School	**Middle School**	**High School**
• Clinging to one predictable peer • Avoiding group games • Withdrawing during unstructured time • Expressing "stomachaches" or sleepiness	• Drifting between social groups • Floating on the edge of conversations • Sitting alone at lunch or during projects • Sudden changes in clothing style or posture	• Perfectionism • Excessive independence • Academic overdrive *or* complete disengagement • Avoiding clubs, sports, and leadership roles

Understanding these patterns helps adults ask better questions and notice what might otherwise be invisible.

The Invisible Masks of Student Isolation

It's easy to spot a student who is acting out. It is much harder to see a student who is disappearing. Educators routinely describe isolated students as:

- quiet
- easy
- compliant
- focused
- independent

Yet beneath these descriptors is often a nervous system signaling, *"I don't feel safe enough to be myself."*

Isolation hides behind:

- **achievement** (straight-A students with no sense of belonging)
- **leadership** (students who can guide others, but cannot trust others)
- **compliance** (students who never cause trouble, but never connect)
- **withdrawal** (students who appear introverted, but are actually lonely)

Isolation is not a personality trait. It is a physiological and emotional state that shapes behavior. Let's look at how isolation manifests in individual cases.

STUDENT STORY

Marcus - The Performer Disappearing in Plain Sight

Marcus, a high-achieving high school junior, checked every academic box. Perfect attendance. Advanced coursework. Quiet, respectful, reliable. Teachers described him as a dream student.

But between classes, Marcus hovered at the edges of peer groups. During collaborative work, he completed tasks independently, even when peers invited him to join. His posture was guarded; his eyes rarely met others'. He wore competence like armor.

One afternoon, a teacher enthusiastically invited him to an after-school filmmaking club. Marcus paused, shrugged, and whispered, "Maybe…but I doubt anyone would even notice if I was there."

The words landed heavily. His academic performance had become a disguise concealing a profound loneliness.

Marcus represents thousands of students who appear calm on the outside but are collapsing on the inside.

Three Archetypes of Hidden Isolation

While isolation looks different for every student, three patterns appear consistently in schools. These archetypes can help educators recognize social disconnection before it becomes entrenched.

1. The Invisible Student

The quiet student who fades, unnoticed

Outward Signs:

- Sits alone or on classroom peripheries
- Doesn't initiate conversation
- Quiet during transitions
- Avoids eye contact
- Rarely expresses needs

Common Adult Assumptions:

- "They're shy."
- "They're independent."

- "They like being alone."
- "No behavior issues = no concerns."

What's Often Underneath:

- Fear of rejection
- Previous social exclusion
- High sensitivity to criticism
- Nervous system hypervigilance
- Masking of loneliness

Insight: During group work, classmates divide themselves quickly. The Invisible Student hesitates, fidgets with materials, then quietly forms a "group of one." Nobody notices. And the student expects nothing more.

2. The Performer

High achiever who uses success as a shield

Outward Signs:

- Exceptional academic performance
- Perfectionism
- Over-preparation
- Excessive organization
- Reluctance to ask for help

Common Adult Assumptions:

- "They're driven."
- "They don't need support."
- "They're responsible."

What's Often Underneath:

- Anxiety about disappointing adults
- Belief that worth = achievement
- Emotional disconnection from peers
- High internal pressure
- Difficulty trusting anyone

Insight: A student receives a 92% on an assignment and panics—not because of the grade itself, but because performance feels like the only safe entry point into belonging somewhere.

3. The Lone Leader

Competent, confident, but emotionally unanchored

Outward Signs:

- Guides group projects
- Well-liked, but not deeply known
- Frequently chosen for leadership roles
- Good at reading the room

Common Adult Assumptions:

- "They're socially strong."
- "They have lots of friends."
- "They're emotionally mature."

What's Often Underneath:

- Difficulty with vulnerability
- Feeling responsible for others' needs
- Fear of being seen as weak
- Shallow friendships despite wide social circles

Insight: A student who helps everyone else through their crises but has no one they feel close enough to confide in when in need.

STUDENT STORY

Serena - The Social Butterfly Who Felt Alone

Serena, an eighth grader, regularly filled the hallways with laughter. Teachers saw her as bubbly and socially successful. She floated among peer groups easily and was constantly surrounded by people. But during an advisory period, she went to the school counseling office and shared with the counselor that none of her friendships felt real. She was "included" everywhere but "connected" nowhere. Her social energy masked an internal truth. She felt unknown, unseen, and unsupported.

Serena's story reveals an essential distinction: ***Being socially active is not the same as belonging.*** Students can appear surrounded yet feel profoundly alone. This is where you come in. By staying attuned to subtle cues, you can be the instrument of early intervention for students suffering in isolation.

Why Diagnosing Disconnection Matters

Recognizing isolation is not only an exercise in empathy, but also a **neurological intervention.**

When Students Experience *Belonging*:

CORTISOL DROPS 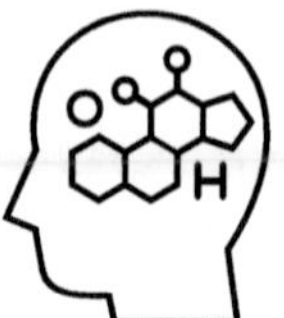

THE AMYGDALA CALMS 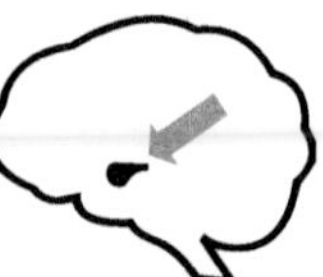

THE PREFRONTAL CORTEX ACTIVATES 

MEMORY, FOCUS, AND PLANNING IMPROVE 

MOTIVATION INCREASES

When Students Feel *Disconnected*:

THEIR BRAINS CONSERVE ENERGY FOR SURVIVAL, NOT LEARNING 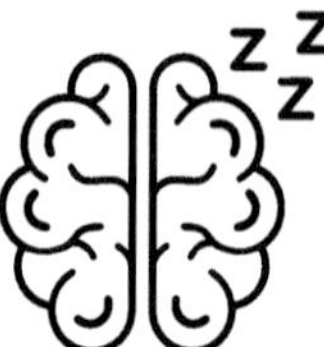

THEY LOSE ACCESS TO CURIOSITY AND CREATIVITY 

THEIR NERVOUS SYSTEMS BECOME RIGID AND REACTIVE 

THEY WITHDRAW OR OVERPERFORM TO COPE 

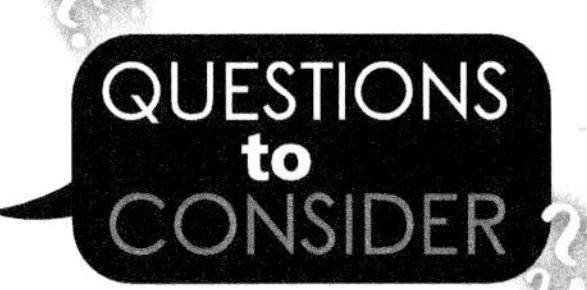

1. How might my assumptions about "maturity," "self-reliance," or being "low maintenance" cause me to overlook student distress?

2. Which students in my care may have risk factors that make isolation more likely?

3. What systems in my school or setting help identify isolated students before academic decline or behavioral escalation occurs?

- **Healthy solitude supports development** when it is voluntary and restorative; isolation occurs when students are physically present but emotionally disconnected.

- **Social presence is not the same as belonging.** Students can be surrounded by peers and still feel unseen or unsupported.

- **Adults may unintentionally reinforce isolation** when they assume that quiet, compliant, or "low-maintenance" students have no needs.

- **Isolation affects brain function.** Belonging regulates the stress response and supports learning, while disconnection can keep students in a defensive state.

- **Early recognition matters.** Without intervention, hidden isolation can become entrenched and shape identity, relationships, and long-term well-being.

Choose one student you rarely interact with.

Offer a simple verbal acknowledgment:

- "I'm glad you're here."
- "I noticed your effort yesterday."
- "You're doing a great job navigating today."

Watch for micro-shifts: eyes softening, posture relaxing, a slight smile.

These micro-moments build neural pathways for trust.

Ask yourself these questions during any routine school day:

- Which students never raise their hands?
- Which students never ask for help?
- Who leaves quickly after class to avoid interaction?
- Who seems tense during group assignments?
- Whose body language softens only when spoken to privately?

Student Name: ____

Hidden Isolation Checklist

Use this checklist during passing periods, lunch duty, classroom transitions, or reflection to spot subtle cues.

Physical/Behavioral Indicators

- [ ] Frequently sits alone
- [ ] Body turned away from peer groups
- [ ] Silent during group dynamics
- [ ] Overly polite or overly agreeable
- [ ] Frequently apologizes

Academic Indicators

- [ ] Perfectionistic tendencies
- [ ] Sudden decrease in depth or effort
- [ ] Works alone even when collaborative options exist

Social Indicators

- [ ] No consistent friendship group
- [ ] Drifts from one cluster to another
- [ ] Avoids lunchrooms or after-school spaces

Emotional Indicators

- [ ] Flat affect
- [ ] Hesitation before speaking
- [ ] Noticeable self-doubt
- [ ] Masked frustration or hidden sadness

The goal is not to label—but to **notice**.

The stakes are high. But with attuned awareness and intentional practice, school adults can interrupt cycles of isolation and reshape neural pathways toward trust.

Once educators begin to recognize the subtle signs of disconnection, the next step is understanding **why** these patterns matter so profoundly. To do that, we must investigate the brain itself. Specifically, we must look at how *belonging* activates neural systems and how *isolation* disrupts them.

Chapter 2 explores the neuroscience behind belonging and how even small interactions reshape the developing brain.

The Neuroscience of Connection

In schools today, you'll find students navigating an endless stream of social cues. Who will I sit with? Does the teacher *see* me? Am I safe here? Do I belong? These questions are not simply emotional; they are **neurological imperatives**.

The human brain is a social organ. From infancy through adolescence (and beyond), the developing nervous system relies on attuned relationships to build the brain architecture that supports learning, regulation, and resilience. When a student feels connected, their brain opens to exploration and curiosity. When they feel excluded, their brain shifts into a protective mode, narrowing its capacity to manage emotion or process information.

Bessel van der Kolk (author of *The Body Keeps the Score*) writes**,** "In the absence of safe relationships, human beings lose their capacity to regulate." Schools can be those safe relationships—**not for one student or some students, but for all students systematically.**

Belonging operates on a loop. This is why belonging is not a "soft" skill. It is a *self-reinforcing* neural practice.

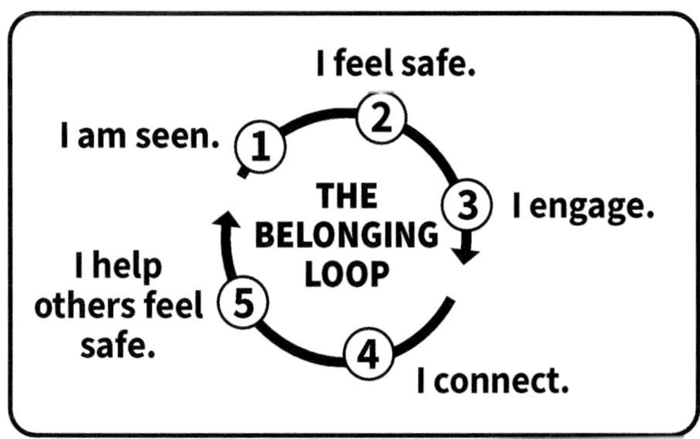

Students who feel connected are more likely to:

- reach out to isolated peers
- help newcomers integrate
- repair conflict with less shame
- mentor younger students
- lower their social defensiveness
- demonstrate more flexible thinking
- take more academic risks

In other words, **belonging doesn't just improve the individual; it improves the whole system.** And this is where the long-term payoff becomes visible.

In this chapter, we unpack the science behind belonging. Not the abstract idea of it—but the **biological reality**. We explore how connection lights up the brain, how isolation shuts it down, and why even brief moments of attuned attention can act as a "neural reset," restoring safety and learning readiness.

The Neuroscience of Belonging in Action

Educators don't need to be neuroscientists to harness the science of connection. They simply need to understand a few key principles and practice them consistently.

For decades, researchers believed cognitive skills such as memory, focus, and problem-solving developed separately from social experiences. We now know that this separation is false. Healthy cognitive functioning is inseparable from relational experience.

The Social Brain in Action

The brain's architecture develops through:

- repeated interactions
- predictable relationships
- emotional attunement
- the sense of being seen and valued

Belonging is so essential that the brain treats it as a survival requirement. The same neural pathways that process *physical pain* are activated when a student experiences social pain or exclusion. In short:

The brain interprets belonging as *safety*.

This single concept can serve to help us reframe our entire approach to the school experience. Let's look at an example of what that's like in a student's life:

The brain interprets disconnection and isolation as *danger*.

STUDENT STORY

Elena - How a Small Connection Rewired Her Learning

When Elena entered seventh grade mid-year, she seemed compliant and self-reliant. She followed rules, completed assignments, and stayed quiet. Many teachers viewed her transition as smooth.

But one of the classroom associates for her grade level noticed small signals:

- minimal eye contact
- inconsistent homework completion
- drifting during transitions
- subtle anxiety in group work

In truth, Elena was overwhelmed. Her family had moved frequently. She didn't know the unspoken rules of this new school. Her nervous system was locked in **hypervigilance**, scanning constantly for threat. Truly engaging in learning was nearly impossible.

The classroom associate mentioned this to one of the school counselors, who immediately offered their support. One simple intervention changed everything. A peer mentor who greeted Elena daily, walked with her to lunch twice a week, and checked in with her once a week in the counselor's office during an advisory period. These predictable interactions helped her nervous system shift from high alert to cautious trust. Her engagement increased. Her affect brightened.

Elena didn't need a complex support plan—she needed **connection**.

This is the neuroscience of belonging in motion.

How <u>Isolation</u> *Disrupts* Brain Function

When students feel unsafe, unseen, or disconnected, the brain activates its survival systems:

1. Amygdala Activation

The amygdala acts like the brain's smoke alarm. When students feel excluded, the amygdala becomes more reactive, scanning intensifies, and neutral interactions can be misinterpreted as threats.

A simple peer glance can feel like judgment. A group assignment can feel like danger. A wrong answer can feel like humiliation.

2. Cortisol Flooding the System

Prolonged social stress triggers cortisol release. Elevated cortisol impairs attention, reduces working memory, decreases problem-solving abilities, and narrows cognitive flexibility.

Even small academic tasks feel overwhelming when the brain is in survival mode.

3. Decreased Prefrontal Cortex Activation

The prefrontal cortex (PFC) is responsible for executive function, such as:

- decision-making
- impulse control
- planning
- empathy
- perspective-taking

During isolation, blood flow shifts away from the PFC and toward areas responsible for protection and threat detection. As a result, students become:

✓ less patient

✓ less reflective

✓ less able to access higher-order thinking

✓ more rigid in their thinking (no gray)

✓ more reactive

✓ more likely to succumb to "easy"

This is why a disconnected student may appear unmotivated or oppositional—they are neurologically restricted.

4. Reduced Dopamine and Oxytocin

Belonging fuels dopamine (engagement, motivation) and oxytocin (trust, bonding). Without these essential chemical reactions happening in the brain, tasks feel meaningless, risks feel dangerous, motivation drops, curiosity diminishes, and school becomes emotionally flat.

Isolation drains the brain's natural reward systems.

In short, chronic isolation:

- shrinks cognitive capacity
- increases emotional volatility
- blocks learning
- distorts perception
- disrupts executive functions

This is not misbehavior. This is neurology.

How <u>Belonging</u> *Amplifies* Brain Function

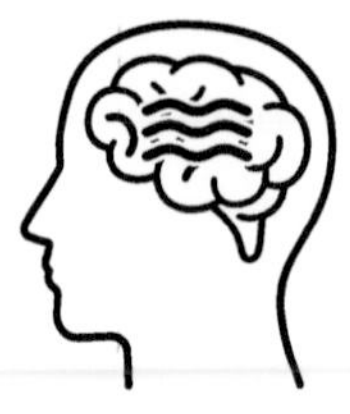

When a student feels safe and connected, the brain shifts into a state researchers call **"optimal learning readiness."**

1. Amygdala Calms

Warm greetings, predictable routines, and attuned interactions reduce amygdala activity. Students become less defensive, more open to challenge, and more flexible

2. Cortisol Drops

Connected students can retain new information, regulate emotions more effectively, stay present, and engage with instruction.

3. Prefrontal Cortex Activates

This reactivation boosts reasoning, planning, reflection, creativity, and empathy. Students regain access to the parts of the brain that make learning possible.

4. Dopamine and Oxytocin Increase

These two chemicals reinforce engagement, motivation, bonding, resilience, and effort over time. A student who feels like they belong is more willing to try even when work is hard.

Note: See the downloadable resources for a comparison chart on isolation vs. belonging and brain function.

Neural Safety Signals

The nervous system responds to brief moments of connection, sometimes in as little as five seconds. This is where neural safety signals come in. A neural safety signal is any short interaction that cues the brain toward safety.

How It Works

Within seconds, attuned human connection increases parasympathetic activation, slows breathing, softens muscle tension, reduces heart rate variability, boosts oxytocin, and shifts the nervous system toward calm.

Examples in Action

- A teacher makes warm eye contact and says, "I'm glad you're here."
- A counselor notices a student's effort: "You worked hard to get here today."
- A coach greets every athlete by name at practice.
- A front office staff member offers a genuine, attentive smile to a nervous parent.
- A bus driver gives a thumbs-up when a student boards the bus.

These neural safety signals accumulate. Over time, they wire the brain for trust and belonging. They are small, consistent interactions that shape neural pathways. They do not require curriculum, funding, or large initiatives. They require *presence*.

Neural Safety Signals Include

- Warm, attuned facial expressions
- Gentle vocal tone
- Correctly pronounced names
- Predictable routines
- Calm adult body language
- Respect for cultural norms around personal space
- Consistent acknowledgment ("I see you")
- Genuine curiosity

Why They Work

The nervous system constantly interprets signals from the environment to determine safety. These signals, called **neuroception**, operate below conscious awareness.

Students are not thinking, *"Does this teacher like me?"* Their nervous system is asking, *"Am I safe with this person?"* Neural safety signals answer that question.

SELF-SCAN: A Practical Reflection for Educators

At the end of a school day, ask yourself:

Who Did I Connect With Today?

- Who received warmth from me? Who did not?
- Who received attention from me only when correcting undesired behavior?
- Who faded into the background of the classroom today?

Who Did I Assume Was "Fine" Without Evidence?

- The student who never asks questions?
- The high achiever who never needs help?
- The quiet one who always sits alone?
- The leader who seems confident but guarded?

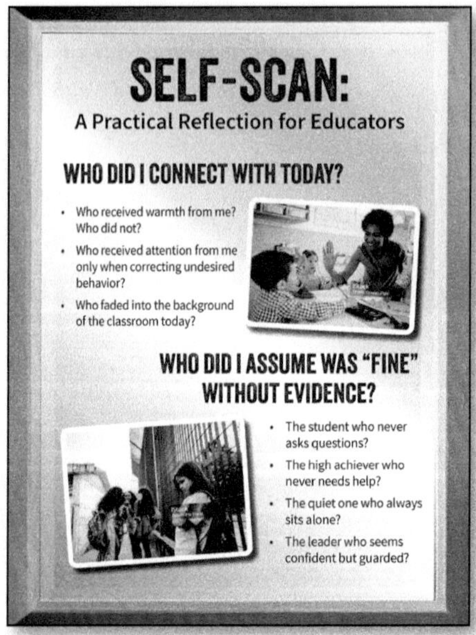

Assumptions often hide the most isolated students. This simple daily scan sharpens an educator's relational attunement.

The Social Synapse

Neuroscience shows that emotional states are contagious. The brain uses a network of mirror neurons to read and replicate facial expressions, tone, posture, affect, and stress levels.

Think about a time when you were in a conversation with someone sitting across from you, whether professional or casual.

- Notice how you sit: legs crossed or uncrossed
- Notice how you place your arms: on the table or in your lap
- Notice your tone of voice: loud and boisterous, or subdued and conspiratorial

Usually, humans imitate those they are near. This is normal, but it also has strong implications:

A single connected student can improve group dynamics.
A single dysregulated student can disrupt them.

A single attuned adult can reset the entire room.
A single dysregulated adult can set the entire room on edge.

Emotional contagion is real and powerful. This is why every student needs at least one adult who serves as a **relational anchor**—a predictably present, emotionally attuned, culturally responsive adult who signals safety.

Anchors can include:

- teachers
- school counselors
- coaches
- paraprofessionals
- office staff
- custodians
- bus drivers
- cafeteria staff
- other school-based support

It's not the role that matters; it's the stability of the relationship and the authenticity of the connection.

What Relational Anchors Do

- Greet consistently
- Provide calm during dysregulation
- Remember important details
- Check in during transitions
- Reflect student strengths
- Offer nonjudgmental presence

Students with strong relational anchors demonstrate higher attendance, stronger executive function skills, fewer discipline referrals, higher GPA, and more resilience. The ultimate goal is for belonging to become a skill students carry beyond the classroom.

When students internalize inclusion, they develop relational resilience, enabling them to seek, create, and sustain meaningful connections throughout life. Relational anchors serve not only as facilitators of immediate belonging but as architects of enduring identity and social competence.

A Culture of Trust

Trust is not an abstract feeling. It is a neurochemical experience shaped by connection. ***Connection literally transforms brain chemistry.*** Based on this understanding, we also know that neuroception does not operate in a cultural vacuum.

Students' nervous systems interpret relational cues based on their lived experiences, family values, community norms, and cultural backgrounds. What signals "I am safe, seen, and respected" to one student may signal "I am being judged, threatened, or misunderstood" to another.

Consider what could happen when school connection initiatives are not culturally responsive. Might educators unintentionally activate a student's threat response instead of their engagement system? In short, cultural responsiveness is not just best practice; it is neuroscience in action.

Let's see what cultural responsiveness may look like in the life of an elementary student recently transferred to a new school.

STUDENT STORY

Hani - Neural Safety in Action

Hani, a fifth grader, was new to the school. He had transferred in mid-year and entered school daily with a rigid posture and clenched fists. He scanned the room constantly. He avoided peers and resisted group work.

His teacher quietly began a ritual. Every morning she greeted him at the door with a steady smile, bowed her head, and with her hand over her heart she repeated the same phrase: **"I'm glad to see you."**

The first week, he avoided eye contact.

The second week, he whispered, "Hello."

The third week, his shoulders softened, and he shyly returned the smile.

Within a month, Hani volunteered to work in a small group for the first time.

Nothing changed academically, yet everything changed neurologically.

How Cultural Cues Affect Neuroception

Below are common examples of behaviors interpreted differently across cultures, along with concrete educator actions:

BEHAVIOR	HOW IT VARIES	EDUCATOR PRACTICE
Eye Contact	• For some cultures, direct eye contact communicates confidence, attention, and respect. • For others, prolonged eye contact may be viewed as challenging, disrespectful, or confrontational—especially from a young person to an adult.	• Avoid demanding eye contact or interpreting lack of it as disengagement or defiance. • Use indicators such as body posture, note-taking, facial expression, and attentiveness instead of eye contact alone to assess student engagement.
Physical Proximity	• Some cultures value closeness, touch, and shared personal space as signs of warmth and connection. • Others view close proximity as intrusive, unfamiliar, or threatening.	• Before entering a student's personal space (e.g., leaning over a desk, touching a shoulder), pause and consider whether you've built relational permission. • When possible, give students a choice: "Would you like to talk here or step into the hallway where it's quieter?"
Public Praise	• Some students feel energized and affirmed when praised publicly. • Others may feel exposed, singled out, or embarrassed.	• Ask students privately how they prefer to receive recognition. • Use a mix of affirmation styles: verbal, written notes, quiet acknowledgments, or group-based celebration.
Individual Questioning	• Some students see being called on individually as a sign of teacher investment. • Others experience it as unwanted spotlighting that may activate social threat or shame.	• Offer the option to respond in ways that feel safe: writing, small groups, turn-and-talks, or passing without penalty. • Normalize choice: "You're always free to pass if you want more time to think."

The Neurological Implication

When a student's cultural norms are ignored or violated, the nervous system interprets interactions as unsafe. This can result in reduced executive functioning, lower levels of participation, emotional withdrawal, defensive behavior, or misinterpretation of student responses as non-compliance.

Conversely, when educators signal respect for cultural context, the nervous system shifts into a ventral vagal state associated with safety, curiosity, belonging, and engagement. Learning becomes more accessible. Relationships deepen. This is not just relational—it is biological. When educators honor a student's cultural frame, they regulate the brain toward connection.

Concrete Practices for Culturally Responsive Neuroception

Educators can strengthen culturally safe connections in many ways:

- **Ask students and families directly** – "What does respect look like in your home?" or "How would you like teachers to interact when giving feedback or redirecting?"
- **Build classroom norms collaboratively** – Invite students to help define what communication, praise, and support should look like.
- **Don't assume sameness** – Replace "fair means the same for everyone" with "fair means everyone gets what they need to feel safe and connect to learning."
- **Check for interpretation, not intention** – If a student withdraws, becomes reactive, or shuts down, consider: "Was a threat response just unintentionally activated?"
- **Expand "warmth" beyond one cultural expression** – Warmth can look like smiles and hugs—or respectful distance and calm tone.
- **Practice cultural humility** – Instead of needing to know "everything about every culture," communicate: "Your experiences matter. Teach me how to support you."

Though teachers are usually well-meaning, what the teacher *intends* does not define connection. Rather, connection is defined by what the student's nervous system experiences. When educators embrace culturally responsive practices, they are not simply being inclusive. Instead, they are optimizing brain states for learning, enhancing relational trust, matching intervention to neurological reality, and validating students' identities, experiences, and histories.

Cultural responsiveness is the bridge between safety and learning. When we honor culture, we activate connection.

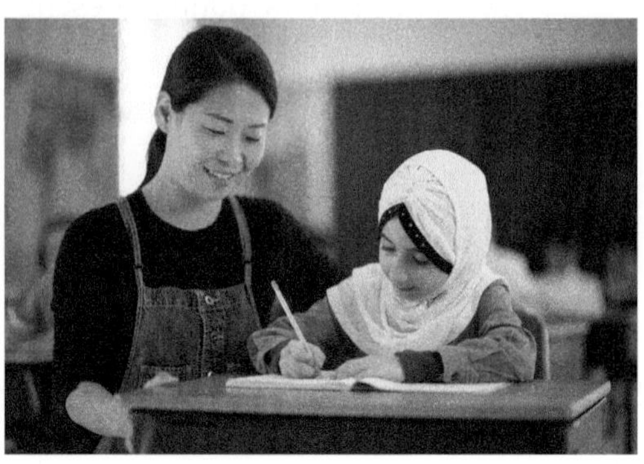

From Isolation to Integration

When educators create connection-rich environments, students demonstrate four predictable neural changes:

1. **Increased Emotional Regulation** – Students stay calmer longer, recover from stress more quickly, and use more adaptive coping strategies.

2. **Strengthened Executive Function** – Students improve in planning, task initiation, self-monitoring, and flexibility.

3. **Enhanced Cognitive Engagement** – Students participate more, take academic risks, ask for help, and show curiosity.

4. **Restored Social Confidence** – Students begin joining groups, forming friendships, trusting adults, and expressing needs.

These changes occur through repeated moments of relational safety.

Practical Strategies for Using Neuroscience in Daily Practice

Educators can integrate brain-based strategies effortlessly into daily routines.

PREDICTABLE CONNECTION ROUTINES

Create rituals:

- Morning greetings
- Class meetings
- Exit tickets that ask about students' day
- Weekly reflection prompts

ATTUNED BODY LANGUAGE

- Open posture
- Soft eye contact
- Relaxed shoulders
- Calm voice
- Slower pace

EMOTIONAL LABELING

Help students name feelings:

- "It sounds like you're frustrated."
- "I see that this is overwhelming."

Labeling reduces amygdala reactivity.

REGULATION MODELING

Model:

- Deep, quiet breathing
- Pauses before reacting
- Self-compassion
- Perspective-taking

Remember: *students mirror the adult nervous system.*

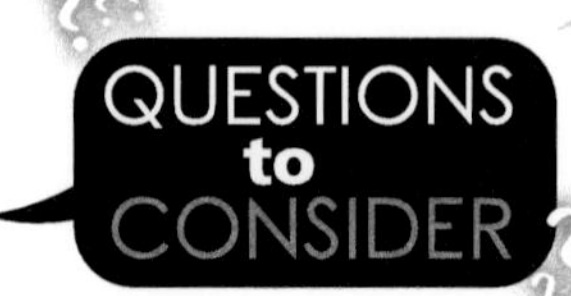

1. What actions or attitudes that I have labeled as "behavior" might instead reflect stress, disconnection, or neurological restriction?

2. In moments of dysregulation, do I focus first on behavior or on regulation and safety?

3. If belonging is foundational for learning, how should that shape instruction, discipline, and support systems?

4. What small, consistent practices could strengthen safety, calm, and connection in my environment?

- **Cognition and connection are intertwined.** Learning, memory, attention, and self-regulation develop through relational experience.

- **Isolation restricts capacity.** Chronic disconnection disrupts executive functioning, distorts perception, and limits learning readiness.

- **The brain reads belonging as safety and disconnection as threat.** This lens reframes many behaviors often labeled as misbehavior.

- **Regulation drives engagement.** When students feel safe and supported, higher-order thinking, curiosity, and participation increase.

- **Emotions are contagious.** Through mirror neuron systems, students mirror the tone, stress, and regulation of the adults around them.

- **Trust develops through predictable relationships.** Consistent routines, authentic interactions, and culturally responsive practices gradually build belonging and resilience.

Predictability Cue

Post the day's agenda visibly. Discuss changes with the class throughout the day. This reduces cognitive load and anxiety.

Micro-Connection

Pause during the day to lower your tone of voice and say a student's name gently before you give an instruction or provide academic feedback.

Co-Regulation Moment

- Sit beside—not across
- Visibly slow your breathing
- Use a soft, steady tone
- Offer one simple choice

Neurologically safe interventions don't have to take a lot of time or take anything out of your already over-extended budget. **Chapter 3** introduces the practice of the **5-Second Neural Reset** and offers practical, powerful tools every educator can use to infuse belonging into daily interactions.

3 The Neural Reset

Let's return to the image of an educator standing in the doorway of a classroom, watching activity in the hallway. Imagine it's right after lunch hour. Students pour through the hallway behind you—some laughing, some sleepy, some anxious, some pretending to be fine, some excited about what comes next. The hallway noise builds, the transition seems chaotic, and the classroom fills quickly. But within minutes, the teacher begins managing materials, assigning tasks, and attending to student needs.

Within this flurry of activity, essential interactions begin to take place. You start to see tiny, largely unnoticed relational moments happening all around:

> A warm greeting.
>
> A nod of recognition.
>
> A quiet "I'm glad you're here."
>
> A coach's calm response to dysregulation.
>
> A teacher who pauses to take a deep breath before reacting.
>
> A school counselor who sits near a student without pressuring them to talk.
>
> A cafeteria staff member who remembers a student's favorite breakfast.

These fleeting experiences, the ones that take only seconds, literally change the brain.

This chapter explores the science and practice of the **5-Second Neural Reset**, a term that reflects the profound neurological impact of brief moments of relational safety.

These micro-interactions calm the nervous system, strengthen executive functioning, and transform the learning environment for all students.

Translating Neuroscience into Daily Practice

A **Neural Reset** is a short interaction, often under five seconds, that sends the message: ***"You're safe. You belong. I see you."***

These interactions activate the parasympathetic nervous system (especially the ventral vagal pathway) and shift the brain out of threat mode. They are grounded in Polyvagal Theory, Affective Neuroscience, and decades of research on Emotional Attunement.

A Neural Reset can include:

- warm eye contact (culturally attuned)
- correct pronunciation of a name
- a brief noticing statement
- a nod that communicates recognition
- a soft smile
- a calm tone
- a grounding phrase
- a gentle co-regulation cue

These small moments reset neuroception, the nervous system's unconscious detection of safety. Small does not mean insignificant. In fact, micro-moments are the most neurologically potent interventions available to educators. Not to mention that they are fast, free, and endlessly customizable.

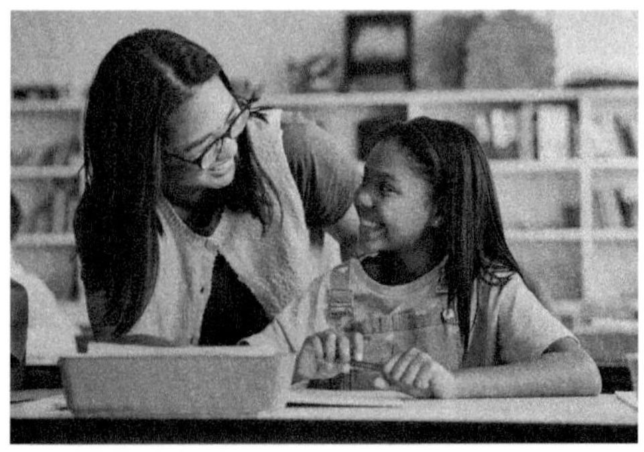

Five seconds of attuned connection is enough to:

- **Calm the Amygdala** – The amygdala is constantly scanning for threat. Warmth and attunement signal safety and decrease activation.
- **Increase Oxytocin** – Even brief eye contact can release oxytocin, the bonding chemical.
- **Boost Dopamine** – Positive acknowledgment triggers dopamine, motivation, and engagement increase.
- **Re-Engage the Prefrontal Cortex** – Once the brain perceives safety, executive functions (planning, attention, reasoning) turn back on.
- **Restore Emotional Balance** – Parasympathetic nervous system activation slows heart rate, reduces cortisol, and supports regulation.

The Result: Students engage more readily, learn more deeply, manage emotions better, and experience school as a place of safety, not survival.

Micro-interactions are the most reliable way to regulate students *proactively*. Yet because they are so small and intuitive, they are often undervalued. Let's take a look at that in action through this staff story.

> A dysregulated, disconnected nervous system cannot access learning.

STAFF STORY

Mr. Alvarez - The Pause That Changed the Day

By the time the second bell rang, Mr. Alvarez already felt behind.

The hallway had been loud. Two students were arguing near his door. His email inbox was full. He still needed to upload attendance, collect yesterday's assignments, and get thirty students settled, all before the lesson could even begin. He felt his jaw tighten as Maya slipped into the room late, as usual, shoulders hunched, eyes down, backpack half-unzipped.

Normally, this was the moment he would correct her.

You're late.
Get started.
We've talked about this.

He felt the urge rise—fast, familiar, automatic. Instead, he paused just long enough to take one slow breath.

When Maya reached her desk, he walked past quietly and said in a calm, even tone, "Good morning, Maya. I'm glad you're here."

It took less than five seconds.

She looked up, surprised. Not startled, just…noticed. She nodded and sat down. No sigh. No eye roll. No tension spiraling outward. Mr. Alvarez felt his own shoulders drop as he turned back to the board.

As the class settled, he noticed something else. The room felt different. Quieter. Not silent, but steadier. Maya opened her notebook instead of freezing. When another student bumped into her chair, she tensed, then exhaled.

Mr. Alvarez realized something important at that moment.

He hadn't lowered expectations.
He hadn't ignored the behavior.
He had regulated *first*.

Throughout the day, he caught himself repeating that same pattern—brief eye contact, a nod during group work, a calm redirection instead of a sharp one. Each interaction was small. Almost forgettable.

But the impact wasn't.

By the end of the week, transitions were smoother. Maya participated more consistently. And just as unexpectedly, Mr. Alvarez felt less depleted. The constant cycle of correction and escalation had softened. Teaching felt more human again.

Later, reflecting with the school counselor, he said, "I didn't change my classroom management. I changed five seconds at a time."

The SAFE Framework: Four Foundations of Daily Connection

The **SAFE Framework** gives educators a simple, practical structure for daily connection. By organizing practices around Safety, Acceptance, Fellowship, and Empathy, this framework helps staff respond to students in ways that calm the nervous system, build belonging, and support learning.

SAFE translates neuroscience into actionable behaviors so educators don't need extra programs or additional time to make an impact. It provides a shared language across school roles, centers regulation before correction, and fosters both student engagement and educator well-being.

In short, SAFE turns brief, intentional micro-interventions into powerful, sustainable practices that help students feel safe, seen, and connected.

AFETY

The nervous system must sense physical and emotional safety before learning can occur.

How educators signal safety:

- predictable routines
- clear expectations
- calm corrections
- attuned body language
- consistent adult behavior

Safety is the foundation of belonging.

**CCEPTANCE**

Students need to feel accepted as individuals, even when behavior must be redirected.

Acceptance signals include:

- recognizing effort
- affirming individuality
- avoiding public shaming
- separating behavior (what you do) from worth (who you are)

Acceptance communicates, "You don't have to earn your place here."

FELLOWSHIP

Belonging grows through intentional, meaningful connections among students. Educators cultivate fellowship within the school community through:

- structured partner and small-group activities
- cooperative learning and collaborative projects
- peer recognition and positive nominations
- social-emotional skill-building opportunities
- shared rituals and traditions that create a sense of "we"
- modeling forgiveness and relational repair, helping students rebuild trust after mistakes or conflict

Fellowship strengthens resilience, reduces isolation, and signals that every student is a valued member of the community.

MPATHY

Empathy builds trust and emotional safety. It helps guide students toward the practices of forgiveness and acceptance of others, and fosters the ability to move past interpersonal mistakes.

Empathetic interactions include:

- reflective listening
- nonjudgmental curiosity
- validating expressed emotions
- patience with dysregulation

Empathy communicates, "Your emotions make sense. You are not alone with them."

Safety is not a feeling we hope students stumble into. It is a daily, intentional, neurologically grounded practice.

Every smile.
Every warm tone.
Every name spoken with care.
Every gentle correction.
Every shared moment of calm.
Every culturally attuned interaction.
Every ritual that says, "You're part of this."

These are not small things. They are the work. They are the conditions that make learning possible. And when the entire school community embraces practices that promote neurological safety, belonging becomes inevitable.

1. How do my own stress signals show up during the school day, and how might they affect students or colleagues?

2. What might students who "push my buttons" reveal about the limits of my own regulation?

3. How do roles of authority influence my willingness to pause, soften, or repair in the moment?

4. How do I signal safety in every interaction, especially when students are dysregulated?

5. Where could my school start building more consistent SAFE practices across settings?

KEY POINTS

- **The nervous system responds to how something is communicated**—tone, pacing, expression, and timing matter as much as words.

- **Neural Resets are proactive strategies** that reduce escalation, correction, and reactive discipline.

- **SAFE translates neuroscience into daily practice** through small, consistent actions that regulate students and strengthen classroom culture.

- **When adults consistently use SAFE practices**, safety and belonging become predictable across the school.

Minute 1 — Greeting: Warm acknowledgment at the door.

Minute 2 — Presence: Sit or stand near a lonely student without pressure.

Minute 3 — Validation: "I see that today feels heavy. You're not alone. I'm here for you."

Minute 4 — Noticing: "I noticed your effort earlier. Thank you."

Minute 5 — Connection Ritual: End class with a communal gesture or phrase.

Schools that intentionally see, know, and anchor every student *before* academic and behavioral pressures recognize a foundational truth of developmental neuroscience:

When safety is unstable, performance collapses.

When safety is a given, potential increases.

Belonging then becomes a prerequisite for learning, regulation, and growth.

Chapter 4 explores how schools move belonging practices from individual effort to systemic reality. It examines the structures, routines, and accountability practices that make relational connection unavoidable, ensuring that every student—not just the most outgoing, the highest achievers, or the loudest voices—is enabled by the environment around them. When belonging becomes a schoolwide commitment rather than a personal one, it stops being aspirational and starts becoming transformational.

4 Cultivating Schoolwide Connection

If you walk into a school that has fully embraced a culture of belonging, the difference is visible before a lesson ever begins. The hallways feel more regulated, the noise more cooperative, the student energy more purposeful. The front office staff greets students by name. Teachers pause to acknowledge students when they walk into the room instead of simply directing them to the first task of the day. Adults make time for what many schools dismiss as "extra"—intentional connection.

Students feel it. Their nervous systems interpret the school climate not as a space where they must prove themselves, defend themselves, or perform perfectly to be accepted, but as a space where they start the day with relational grounding.

This is not accidental. Belonging never emerges by hope alone; it emerges through **design.**

When Belonging is the System, Not the Exception

Belonging, in neurological terms, is not a preference. It is a **human requirement**, one the brain treats as essential, just as it treats the requirements for food or shelter. Students who do not experience belonging are not simply emotionally discouraged—they experience cognitive, regulatory, and physiological impairment.

Many educators believe belonging is something some students "have" and others "lack," a variable that is dependent on personality, social skill, achievement, or behavior. But this way of thinking assumes belonging is primarily about *student effort* rather than **adult design.**

In schools **without** systemic connection structures, belonging depends entirely on luck:

- the right teacher
- the right peer group
- the right club
- the right year

Students who happen to form even one strong relationship thrive. Students who don't may drift through years of schooling, emotionally invisible. And because isolated students often present as compliant, quiet, high-achieving, or self-sufficient, their disconnection remains unnoticed until it emerges as depression, school refusal, intense perfectionism, or disengagement.

When schools institutionalize connection, the equation changes. Students don't have to **work to belong.** Belonging becomes the default experience. Let's look at a school that chooses connection with a purpose.

SCHOOL STORY

Ridgeview Middle

Ridgeview Middle noticed a trend. Sixth graders transitioning from elementary school were arriving anxious, disconnected, and often walking the halls alone. The school counselor piloted a simple change by instituting a program she called "Belonging Ambassadors," a rotating team of seventh grade students who regularly checked in with new students and welcomed peers with smiles, waves, and morning check-ins.

The results were measurable:

- 6th grade disciplinary referrals dropped
- Students self-reported fewer "bad days"
- Lunch seating patterns shifted to include more mixed groups

One sixth grader put it in simple but profound words, "When someone waves to me every morning, it makes it harder to stay mad all day." That sentence is a neuroscience curriculum in itself.

A friendly wave is not just a wave. It is:

- a neuroceptive cue of safety
- a signal of being seen
- a relational anchor
- a start-of-day neural reset

Schools that understand this stop treating connection as sentimental. Instead, they treat it as **instructional infrastructure.**

Belonging in a Tiered Framework

Schools are increasingly fluent in tiered academic and behavioral intervention systems. What many schools have not yet fully embraced is the need for **tiered relational support**.

When schools apply a Multi-Tiered System of Supports (MTSS) lens to belonging, the goal becomes:

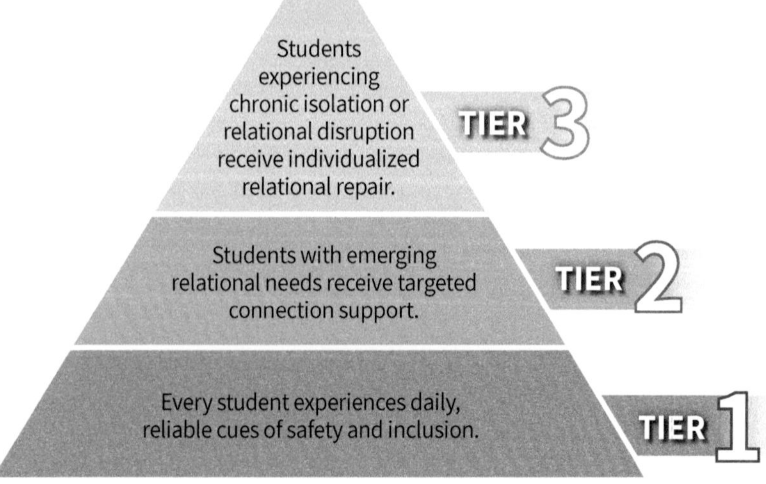

Here is what this looks like in practice:

TIER 1
Universal Systems That Normalize Belonging

Tier 1 systems assume:

- no student should be responsible for creating their own safety net
- adults build predictable relational infrastructure
- connection is woven into instruction, transitions, staff culture, and leadership

Tier 1 structures include:

- daily morning greetings
- open-door advisory periods
- peer acknowledgment systems
- staff rituals
- gratitude practices
- intentional hallway presence
- lunchtime connection opportunities
- "you matter here" visual reinforcements

These practices do not require new curriculum—they require **intentional adult presence.**

Neural Impact of Tier 1 Practices:

- lower cortisol
- increase oxytocin and serotonin
- activate frontal lobe processing
- reduce vigilance
- sustain engagement

In other words, Tier 1 systems protect the brain **before the crisis happens.**

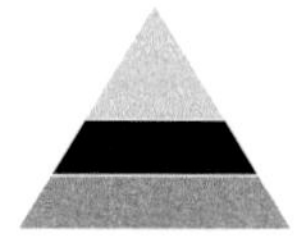

TIER 2
Targeted Supports That Help Students Practice Connection

Some students need **structured relational scaffolding** to succeed—just as they would receive targeted reading intervention if foundational literacy skills were weak.

Tier 2 relational supports:

- "Belonging Ambassador" programs
- lunch buddy groups
- student mentoring
- social skills or emotional literacy small groups
- structured Relational Anchor check-ins
- guided peer practice

These interventions transform "I don't know how to belong in a group" into "I am learning the steps, in real time, with coaching and safety."

Tier 2 in Practice - Belonging Ambassadors

One of the most powerful Tier 2 structures schools can implement is a **Belonging Ambassador** program. Belonging Ambassador programs invite students to become co-creators of school culture. In this intervention, students are trained to take responsibility for expanding the relational fabric of the school.

Belonging Ambassadors:

- welcome new peers
- invite isolated students into shared experiences
- join students who often walk alone
- offer classroom "buddy" support
- monitor who is drifting socially

They are not disciplinarians. They are not hall monitors. They are peers who **notice what adults sometimes miss.** This is not sentimental. This is grounded in neuroscience.

For schools wanting to institutionalize student-led connection work, a Belonging Ambassador model is one of the highest-yield investments.

Below is a structure many schools use successfully.

Step 1: Recruitment

Schools identify students who:

- notice others
- practice empathy
- see students who are overlooked
- can be trusted with confidentiality
- represent diverse social groups

Recruitment signals, "Leadership is not only for the loud, confident, or high-achieving. Leadership is for those who build community."

Step 2: Initial Training (30–60 Minutes)

Core skills:

- how to spot subtle social withdrawal
- how to approach peers respectfully
- how to check on someone without prying
- how to receive rejection without taking it personally
- how to elevate concern to an adult

An example student script:

> *"Hey, want to sit with us today?"*
> *"No pressure, just know you're welcome anytime."*

It's important to recognize that Ambassadors are not expected to "fix" their peers. Their role is to **notice, invite, include, and alert adults when a student may need more support.**

Step 3: Ongoing Supervision

Bi-weekly or monthly:

- check-ins with an adult sponsor
- group problem-solving
- ambassador sharing
- counselor support

This ensures:

- students feel supported
- adults stay informed
- ambassadors don't emotionally overextend
- momentum doesn't fade

What Belonging Ambassadors Notice That Adults Can't

Students see:

- who stands alone in the restroom
- who gets quietly excluded in partner work
- who is chronically absent from social space
- who sits alone at lunch but pretends not to be bothered
- who stops laughing at jokes that used to delight them

When adults and students share relational intelligence, belonging goes from **aspiration to architecture.**

Neural Impact of Tier 2 Intervention:

- dopamine increases through positive social success
- the brain begins associating peer interaction with reward rather than risk
- prefrontal access increases

Tier 2 interventions like Belonging Ambassador programs teach the brain that **connection can succeed.**

Adolescent brains are deeply shaped by peer experiences and are wired for social approval. They are more influenced by student messages than adult ones. When a peer says, "Come sit with us," the brain receives a stronger regulatory signal than if an adult said it. Belonging Ambassadors institutionalize noticing.

TIER 3
Individualized Relational Repair

Tier 3 becomes necessary when:

- a student has experienced relational rupture
- there has been repeated exclusion

- trauma history impacts social functioning
- a break in trust has occurred
- student is returning from suspension, hospitalization, or extended absence

Tier 3 is not about discipline—it is about **relational reconstruction.**

Tier 3 interventions include:

- restorative conversations
- family partnership conferences
- home visits
- individualized "anchor adult" assignments
- stepwise re-entry plans

Neural Impact of Tier 3 Intervention:

- helps rewire social pain circuits
- rebuilds trust and connection
- changes relational expectations from "People are dangerous" to "Connection can be safe."

Tier 3 intervention aims to prove that belonging is not something students earn, it is something they are **repaired back into.**

Systematically Seeing Disconnection Before It Becomes Damage

Most schools do not lack caring adults, but they do lack **relational visibility.** Students who are drifting socially or sinking emotionally often do so quietly. Without intentional structures that surface relational data, the only students who trigger adult attention are the ones whose distress becomes loud enough to disrupt instruction or routines.

But isolation *is* a data point. Schools can measure belonging the same way they measure reading fluency, course failures, or attendance—through routine, predictable systems that reveal who is connected, who is not, and who needs immediate relational scaffolding.

Connection doesn't always disappear with dramatic withdrawal. More often, it fades in small ways:

- a student begins arriving late only to one class
- a student no longer raises their hand
- a lunch table slowly empties around one individual
- a student stops participating in group work

These are not "minor behavior concerns," they are **early neurological alerts.** "Something is overwhelming my ability to stay socially present."

When schools track these patterns as belonging indicators, not just disciplinary data, teams are able to intervene months before a crisis emerges.

Connection Mapping: A Schoolwide Relational Audit

A **Connection Map** is a simple but powerful visual tool that asks:

- Which students feel they have at least one trusted adult on campus?
- Which adults believe they are intentionally connected to specific students?
- Where do we see alignment—and where do we see students with no anchors?

The process is straightforward:

1. **Students complete a short voluntary survey:**
   - "Who at school notices when you're having a hard day?"
   - "Who could you talk to if you needed help?"
   - "Can you name one adult here that you could trust personally?"

2. **Staff complete a parallel form:**
   - "List five students you regularly and intentionally notice and check on."

3. **Data is layered together, then the school looks for:**

- students who appear on no adult lists
- students who believe no adult knows them
- students who rely on only one Anchor
- strong clusters of belonging
- grade-level discrepancies

This process often reveals the most surprising truth in the work of schoolwide belonging:

Students who appear the most stable academically are often the ones most relationally alone.

Quiet, compliant students—particularly those who have learned that invisibility keeps them safe—regularly surface as having no relational ties at all.

In one middle school, a Connection Mapping process revealed that 29% of students on the honor roll could not name a single adult they personally trusted. Not one. Their academic performance had masked their emotional isolation.

Once schools can **see** these students, they can respond.

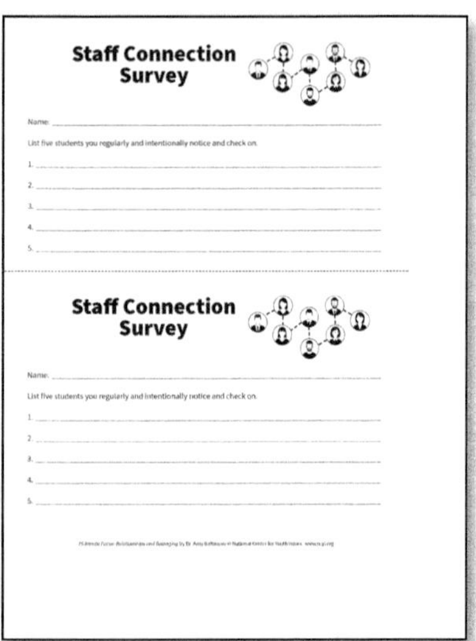

Advocating for Belonging in Data-Driven Environments

Schools today are under enormous pressure to measure:

- reading growth
- math proficiency
- graduation rate
- chronic absenteeism
- behavioral incidents
- college and career readiness

The list goes on and on. In this context, belonging can sometimes be dismissed as "nice, but optional." Yet belonging is not in competition with academic performance; belonging is the **precondition** for academic performance.

No amount of instructional finesse can override a nervous system in survival mode. But educational systems pay attention when schools communicate belonging as:

- a return on investment
- a performance enhancer
- a retention strategy
- a behavior stabilizer
- a college and workforce readiness factor

The Indicators of Long-Term Impact

Belonging is not a nebulous feeling or a motivational slogan. It is observable, measurable, and assessable. Schools that intentionally cultivate connection look for specific **behavioral, emotional,** and **structural indicators** that tell them the culture is shifting at the nervous-system level.

These indicators can be seen in:

✓ Students and their behaviors
✓ Adults and their interactions

✓ Systems and their consistency

✓ Data patterns across time

Let's look at each.

Student-Level Indicators

When belonging takes root, student behavior fundamentally changes—not because rules have become stricter, but because the brain is operating in a different state.

IMPROVED SELF-REGULATION

Students demonstrate:

- faster recovery after conflict
- willingness to take responsibility
- lower reactivity
- fewer fight / flight / freeze responses
- increased capacity to pause before responding

This indicates that the prefrontal cortex—not the amygdala—is leading more of the day.

INCREASED ENGAGEMENT AND PARTICIPATION

Belonging reduces fear of embarrassment, criticism, or rejection. Students who once stayed silent might now:

- answer questions
- ask for clarification
- attempt challenging tasks
- share opinions
- participate in group conversation
- take academic risks

The brain is learning, "I can be visible here and still be safe."

MORE WILLINGNESS TO SEEK HELP

One of the clearest markers that a student feels secure is that they ask for assistance before they fail. In insecure environments, students avoid support because:

- asking makes them vulnerable
- struggle feels like a threat
- being seen equals risk

In belonging-rich schools, asking for support is normalized as:

- maturity
- strength
- part of the learning cycle

PEER PRO-SOCIAL BEHAVIOR

As belonging grows, students begin offering connection—not just receiving it. Signs include:

- students checking on peers when distressed
- voluntarily inviting others into groups
- modeling emotional language
- supporting classmates during struggle
- celebrating each other's successes

Students who experience compassion become more compassionate. This is the recursive nature of connection. Belonging begets belonging.

Adult-Level Indicators

A school cannot be deeply connected for students if adults are brittle, burned out, or relationally isolated. When belonging takes root, educators begin to change, too.

ADULTS BECOME LESS REACTIVE

Staff show:

- fewer power struggles
- lower levels of emotional escalation
- increased use of calm tones
- ability to stay present in conflict
- curiosity before correction
- assumption of positive intent

This is not accidental; it is increased nervous-system capacity.

INCREASED COLLABORATION AND REDUCED PROFESSIONAL ISOLATION

When teachers feel safe:

- they share strategies
- ask for help
- plan together
- problem-solve collectively
- step in for one another

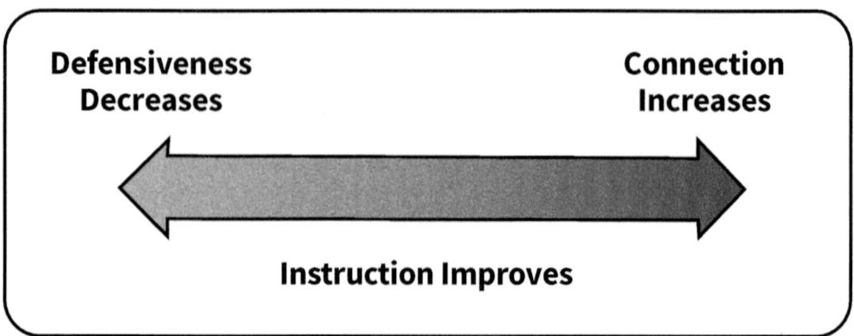

ADULTS MODEL REPAIR

A powerful indicator of a connection culture is an increase in the use of this simple sentence, "I realize I wasn't at my best earlier. I'm sorry."

Students hear:

- mistakes can be fixed
- relationships don't end when someone slips
- adults are also learning
- accountability can be humane

When adults model vulnerability, students become less ashamed of imperfection.

ADULTS SEEK PURPOSE, NOT JUST SURVIVAL

In disconnected environments, adults use language like:

- "I just have to get through this year."
- "One more month until break."
- "I'm just trying to make it."

In connection-rich environments, language shifts to:

- "Look what my students accomplished today."
- "Here's what I'm learning about them."
- "I'm seeing so much growth."

Educators reconnect with **their why**—and this is a neurological transformation too.

System-Level Indicators

When belonging becomes structural rather than personality-driven, you see evidence in the system:

BELONGING APPEARS IN LEADERSHIP AGENDAS

If belonging is real, it becomes a **standing item**, not a bonus topic.

Agenda items look like:

- Which students still lack an adult connector?
- Which staff members need relational support?
- Who has disappeared emotionally or behaviorally this month?
- What belonging practices are we strengthening?

Schools measure what they value.

If belonging is not measured, it is optional.

If it is measured, it becomes mission-critical.

COMMON LANGUAGE ACROSS CLASSROOMS

Students hear consistent messages such as:

- "Let's regulate first, then work the problem."
- "Talk to me about what emotion you are feeling right now."
- "I believe in you, and we can get through this together."

Even small phrases repeated across classrooms function as regulatory anchors.

PREDICTABLE REPAIR PROTOCOLS

Students know:

- what happens after conflict
- the process is safe
- the adult will not shame them
- the relationship remains intact

This predictability lowers chronic stress and increases trust.

ONBOARDING INCLUDES CONNECTION

In maturity, the system:

- teaches new staff and substitutes the belonging model
- introduces students transferring mid-year to students and adults who will intentionally check in
- has a plan so that *no one becomes invisible*

A connection culture that disappears when new people arrive is not yet systemic.

Data-Level Indicators

Decades of research show that students who feel known and connected:

- attend school more regularly
- demonstrate stronger focus and working memory
- persist longer on challenging academic tasks
- exhibit lower rates of suspension and disengagement
- have higher long-term motivation
- participate more voluntarily
- choose healthier peer relationships
- ask for help sooner

None of these outcomes requires "better kids." They require **better neurobiological conditions for learning**.

DISCIPLINE DATA

Connection-rich schools typically see:

- fewer office referrals
- fewer high-intensity behaviors

- fewer repeated offenses
- reduced suspensions
- increased use of restorative practices

Not because adults tightened control, but because students' brains stopped needing to defend themselves all day long.

ATTENDANCE

When students feel connected, the question shifts from "Why should I go to school?" to "Who will notice if I don't?"

Attendance increases not from enforcement, but from attachment.

ACADEMIC GROWTH

When emotional labor decreases, cognitive capacity increases. Schools see:

- higher rates of task completion
- stronger displays of executive functioning skill
- growth in literacy and math
- increased stamina for engaging in learning activities
- improved resilience during challenging tasks

CLIMATE SURVEY DATA

When the systemic focus is on connection, student survey responses shift from:

"Teachers don't understand me."

"I feel alone at school."

"I stay quiet to avoid attention."

to:

"I have adults I trust."

"I can show up as myself."

"People notice when I'm not okay."

"My school believes in me."

Solicit student feedback regularly and adapt practices based on their experiences. Communicate to them "You said, we heard" and explain the changes made on their behalf. Students internalize belonging more deeply when they see that their voices influence the environment over time.

How to Make the Case in Three Minutes

When educators need to justify relational investment, they can point to:

ACADEMIC IMPACT

Connected students:

- attend more
- participate more
- persist longer
- demonstrate higher executive functioning

BEHAVIORAL IMPACT

Belonging reduces:

- office referrals
- classroom disruptions
- power struggles
- emotional reactivity

MENTAL HEALTH IMPACT

Secure relational anchors:

- decrease anxiety symptoms
- support emotion regulation
- reduce student isolation and hopelessness

WORKFORCE CONNECTION

Employers report that the top workplace skills are relational:

- communication
- collaboration
- emotional regulation
- resilience under pressure

Belonging builds the foundation for success in all of those areas.

Data are powerful on their own, but numbers with narrative shift school culture. Instead of saying, *"Students feel more connected this year,"* say:

> *"Since implementing morning greetings building-wide, discipline referrals dropped by 18%, chronic absenteeism decreased by 9%, and the number of students with zero adult connections fell from 41 to 6."*

Pair that with a student quote, "I used to arrive and feel like no one would notice if I was gone. Now someone says good morning every day," and the data then becomes undeniable. Stories make it human. Together, they make belonging **strategic**, not sentimental.

A three-sentence summary that educational leaders often find compelling may go something like this:

> **Belonging is not a wellness initiative.**
> **Belonging is a learning readiness intervention.**
> **When the nervous system is regulated, performance increases.**

This is not a "soft skill."
This is a **prerequisite skill for life readiness.**

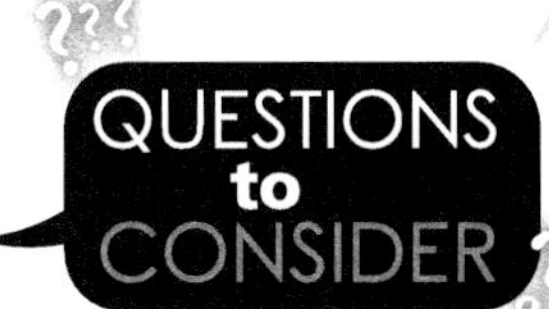

1. How clearly do we define belonging across Tier 1, Tier 2, and Tier 3 supports?

2. Where could we intentionally leverage peer influence to strengthen connection and motivation?

3. What data could we use as early indicators of belonging, and how do we identify students who lack a trusted adult on campus?

KEY POINTS

- **Belonging is perceived before instruction begins.** Students read relational cues in hallways, classrooms, and offices before any academic task.

- **Adult behavior sets the nervous system climate.** Simple, consistent actions such as greeting students by name, pausing for acknowledgment, and offering relational cues that signal safety and support regulation.

- **Belonging requires a tiered approach.** Universal connection is not enough; some students need targeted and individualized relational support.

- **Peer-mediated strategies are powerful.** Programs like Belonging Ambassadors leverage adolescents' sensitivity to peer influence to make connection feel rewarding.

- **Belonging can be measured.** Schools can track relational connection with the same intentionality as attendance, grades, or behavior to identify students who are unanchored.

- **Belonging is both relational and strategic.** When intentionally reinforced and repaired, belonging supports learning readiness and measurable school outcomes.

Select a building-level team that will intentionally observe once per week during arrival:

- What does a student or adult *experience* walking in right now?
- What school staff behaviors are visible?

  Warm greetings? Eye contact? Names used?
  Or: Directives? Rushing? Correction? Supervision-only?

Quick Capture (on a Sticky Note):

- One thing that signals **safety/belonging**
- One thing that signals urgency/performance/compliance

Ask the team to post these anonymous observations in a staff area, such as above the copy machine or near the microwave, so that staff can celebrate and reflect.

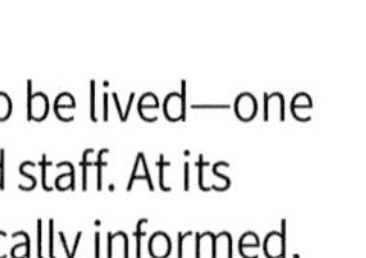

Belonging is not a program to be implemented, but a practice to be lived—one that is sustained through the daily actions of school leaders and staff. At its core, the work of connectedness is deeply relational, neurologically informed, and profoundly impactful. It shapes not only how students feel in a school environment but how ready their brains are to engage, learn, and grow.

Chapter 5 explores how this work does not begin at the school door; it is first cultivated in the home. There, parents and families lead by providing early experiences of safety, stability, and connection, and lay the foundation for how students show up in classrooms and relationships. With intention and consistent practice, educators can build on that foundation, creating moments of safety and connection that regulate the nervous system, strengthen belonging, and ultimately transform a student's experience of school.

When Leadership Sets the Nervous System

Parents and Families

The conditions for learning begin long before students enter a school building. A culture of belonging is first shaped in the home, where parents and families establish an emotional climate that signals safety, stability, and connection to a child's developing brain.

When children consistently experience predictable routines, supportive relationships, and emotional regulation from the adults around them, their nervous systems learn how to interpret normal, daily situations as safe and manageable rather than threatening. This general sense of safety builds resilience, strengthens attention, memory, problem-solving, and self-regulation, all of which are essential capacities for learning.

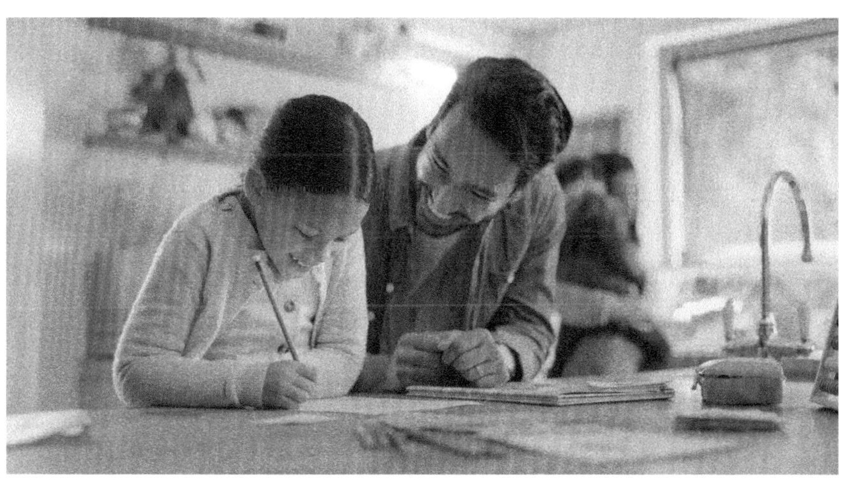

Below is a poster you can send to families with practical tips that can help a child regulate their nervous systems.

10 Ways to Help Your Child Regulate Their Nervous Systems

As a parent or caregiver, you are your child's first experience of safety and belonging. The ten practices below are simple, daily ways to support your child's nervous system and their ability to learn, connect, and grow.

1. CREATE PREDICTABLE ROUTINES

Regular times for waking, meals, homework, and bedtime help children's brains feel safe because they know what to expect. Even simple routines like a nightly check-in or reading together before bed create stability.

2. PRACTICE CALM, REGULATED RESPONSES

Children often mirror the emotional tone of adults. When parents pause, speak calmly, and model problem-solving during stressful moments, they help regulate their child's nervous system.

3. PRIORITIZE DAILY CONNECTION

Spend a few minutes each day in undistracted interaction—talking, playing, or simply listening. Small, consistent moments of attention communicate that the child is valued and seen.

4. NAME AND VALIDATE EMOTIONS

Helping children identify and talk about their feelings ("It looks like you may feel frustrated") teaches emotional awareness and shows that emotions are safe to express.

5. ESTABLISH FAMILY RITUALS

Shared meals, weekend traditions, playing a sport together, etc. create repeated experiences of belonging and togetherness.

6. COMMUNICATE EXPECTATIONS CLEARLY AND CONSISTENTLY

Children feel safer when boundaries and expectations are predictable and proactively explained with respect. Sudden, reactive punishment makes children feel less safe.

7. STAY CONNECTED WITH THE SCHOOL COMMUNITY

Regular communication with teachers and school staff helps children experience continuity between home and school environments.

8. ASK CHILDREN ABOUT THEIR EXPERIENCE

Simple questions like "What was the best part of your day?" or "Did anything feel hard today?" invite reflection and strengthen trust.

9. MODEL BELONGING AND RESPECT

How parents talk about others—neighbors, teachers, classmates—teaches children what empathy and community look like.

10. REPAIR AFTER CONFLICT

When disagreements happen, apologizing, reconnecting, and talking through what happened shows children that relationships can recover and remain safe.

15-Minute Focus: Relationships and Belonging by Dr. Amy Baltimore © National Center for Youth Issues www.ncyi.org

Children do not need perfect environments; they need repeated experiences of safety, predictability, and caring relationships. Over time, these small interactions strengthen trust, emotional regulation, and a deep sense of belonging that supports learning and well-being.

As students transition from home to school, the presence or absence of belonging continues to shape their readiness to engage. When schools partner with families and reinforce these conditions through welcoming relationships, predictable environments, and relational support, students are more likely to feel secure, participate fully, and access the higher-order thinking needed for academic success. In this way, belonging becomes not simply a cultural value but a neurological foundation for learning.

School Leadership

In every school, the leadership sets the relational climate. If school leaders:

- greet students at the front doors,
- show calm in stress,
- acknowledge staff openly,
- demonstrate patience,
- and are physically present,

the nervous systems of adults and students settle.

However, if school leaders primarily:

- operate from urgency,
- communicate only in correction,
- move reactively,
- or reflect unpredictability,

the nervous systems of adults and students stay activated. The tone of a school is rarely set in the classroom first; it radiates from leadership outward.

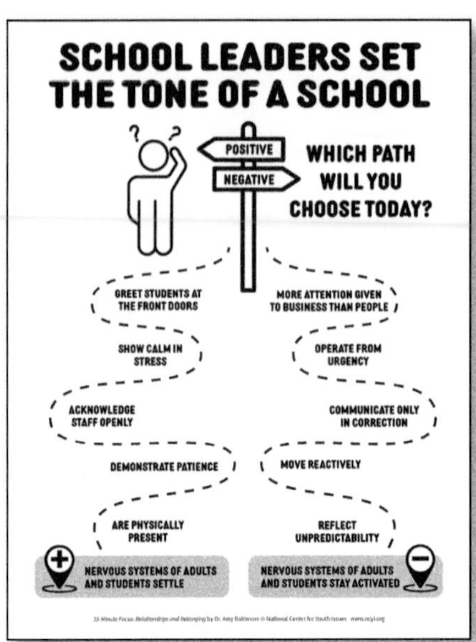

SCHOOL STORY

Ridgeview Revisited

Let's go back to the middle school we visited in chapter 4. After seeing the impact the Belonging Ambassadors made on incoming 6th graders, Principal Sharp initiated the "Morning Greeting Crew" as the next layer of relational connection practices at Ridgeview. Every day, she stood at the front door with other members of the school leadership team, greeting students as they arrived for the day.

Within a semester, teachers began greeting students at their own classroom doors and added three minutes of intentional belonging rituals at the start and end of class. School counselors began short "notice rounds," walking hallways during class changes to pay attention to who was fading socially. The assistant principals redesigned their walkthrough protocol to include relational observations, not just instructional ones.

By spring, office discipline referrals dropped, lunchtime seating patterns diversified, peer conflicts resolved faster, and fewer students were referred for crisis counseling.

The most telling shift was student language. When school counselors interviewed students at the end of the year, one said, "Before, I thought everyone already knew each other and I was just on the out. Now I know other people were isolated, too. We learned how to *see* each other. Coming to school is so much better now."

Belonging became something Ridgeview was **teaching** rather than something they merely hoped would happen.

Practical Tools School Leaders Can Use Tomorrow

Belonging should not require a multi-year rollout, a new grant, or a burdensome new program. Intentional connection can start tomorrow with low-prep, high-impact practices that increase relational visibility and provide consistent safety cues for students' nervous systems.

Here are rapid-deployment tools school administrators can implement immediately.

 1. The "Five Greetings" Challenge

Encourage every adult in the building to commit to **greeting five students a day by name**, making eye contact, and offering a brief relational cue:

"Good morning."

"Glad you're here."

"How's your day going?"

This takes less than sixty seconds, yet regularly triggers:

- oxytocin release
- nervous system settling
- increased classroom cooperation
- perception of belonging

If one teacher greets five students a day, that's 25 students a week, 100 per month, and 900 per school year. Multiply that by every adult in the building and belonging scales exponentially.

 ## 2. "Two-by-Ten" Relationship Intervention

Research shows that spending **two minutes a day for ten days in a row** in positive, non-corrective conversations with struggling students dramatically improves:

- cooperation
- behavior
- engagement
- attitudes toward school

The Structure: Two minutes of student-led conversation with no agenda and no correcting for ten consecutive school days.

It is astonishing how often students improve simply because "Someone is choosing to invest in me without waiting for me to earn it."

 ## 3. Temperature Checks at the Door

These support the ritual of adults greeting students as they enter the building and ask: "Thumbs up, thumbs sideways, thumbs down? How's your energy today?"

This is fast, nonverbal, and reveals:

- who is dysregulated
- who may need co-regulation
- who needs support before instruction

Some teachers keep sticky notes ready for students to write their names and stick on their desks:

- green ("I'm okay")
- yellow ("I might need a check-in")
- red ("I'm having a tough day")

This tiny routine changes the emotional physics of the school. Students no longer carry invisible stress into academic tasks.

 ## 4. The Notice Round

Once a week, members of the school leadership staff briefly walk through hallways, the cafeteria, or advisory areas and ask themselves:

- Who is physically alone?
- Who enters quietly and leaves quietly every day?
- Who seems tired, deflated, or socially withdrawn?
- Who is fading from participation?

These observations become data that provide talking points in student support meetings, which lead to Tier 2 and Tier 3 referrals.

We cannot support students we do not see. Noticing is intervention.

 ## 5. The Classroom - "Four Belonging Questions"

Administrators intentionally provide time and support for classroom teachers to meet with each of their homeroom students and ask (anonymously or openly—depending on their comfort level):

"Do you feel I know you?"

"Do you feel you belong in this class?"

"Is there someone here who notices how you're doing?"

"What could we change to increase a feeling of belonging?"

This data becomes:

- lesson design guidance
- classroom rituals
- advisory topics
- team discussions

Through this practice, students often provide solutions adults hadn't considered:

"I wish we switched partners more."

"It's uncomfortable that the same group always gets picked first."

"I don't know anyone in here yet."

If we ask students what they need, they will tell us.

School-Based Staff

Adults in a school building also need to know they belong. School staff cannot give students what they themselves are running out of. Adults who feel:

- unseen,
- unappreciated,
- isolated,
- and emotionally exhausted,

lose the capacity to co-regulate students.

When educators are dysregulated:

- tone sharpens
- patience shortens
- students are more frequently interpreted as "defiant" or "disengaged"
- adult nervous systems broadcast stress

And because emotional states are contagious (thanks to mirror neurons), entire classrooms can shift based on one dysregulated adult.

This is not blame—it is biology.

School leadership teams must invest in **adult belonging** with the same insistence they bring to student support.

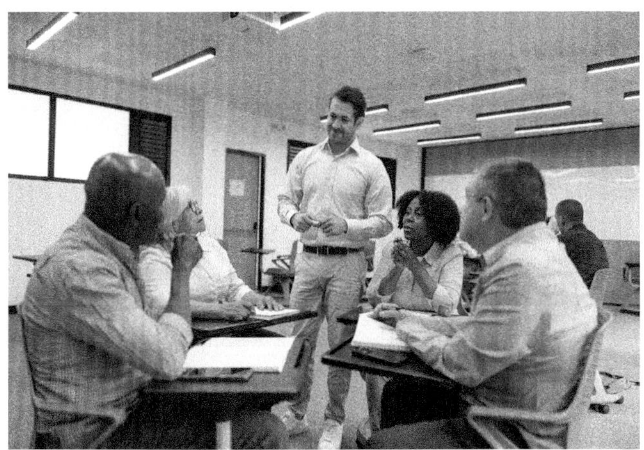

Even minimal rituals have a powerful impact:

- 30-second morning staff check-ins with intentional follow-up
- Friday "wins and grins" messages
- Actively noticing emotional labor and providing space for decompressing and self-regulating
- Peer-to-peer buddy systems for new hires, with intentional leadership support
- Shared relational language

Adults who feel heard and held build classrooms where students feel heard and held. Adults who feel alone struggle to create conditions they do not experience themselves. If we want regulated students, we must support regulated adults.

One simple shift changes everything. In leadership team meetings, add a recurring check-in, "Who is drifting that we need to circle around?"

When school leaders regularly ask themselves this question:

- isolated school professionals disappear less
- struggling professionals surface earlier
- teams work more collaboratively
- ownership is shared and accountability deepens

A school leadership team moves from "That teacher is struggling," to "What have we done to connect with that teacher?" That single change, **from blame to responsibility**, reshapes school culture.

Reflection Prompts for School Leaders

Which adults in the building appear successful but are relationally disengaged?

____
____
____
____

How many adults in our building seem to isolate themselves?

____

If staff were asked to anonymously list the five students they are intentionally "holding," which staff members would have no students listed or would not respond at all?

____
____
____
____

What is one Tier 1 ritual you could begin this week to connect with the adults in the building?

____
____
____
____

How might the leadership team formally track belonging data among the staff?

____
____
____
____

Reflection Prompts
for School Staff

When was the last time you intentionally noticed a quiet staff member who never asks for help?

What relational practices help you feel valued—and how could you extend the same experience to someone you work with?

Which of your colleagues are "good at being invisible"?

Who have you noticed silently asking for help? What could you do to make a connection?

Belonging is not the result of personality, chance, or luck; it is the result of **architecture.** When schools design relational systems with the same seriousness they apply to academic interventions:

- student behavior stabilizes
- emotional regulation improves

- learning accelerates
- connection becomes normalized
- isolation becomes preventable

Schools change when adults shift from "I hope students feel connected" to "We are committed to building systems that ensure students experience connection." That shift transforms belonging from a possibility to a promise.

School Counselors

Because school counselors often work across grade levels and systems, they hold a panoramic view of student experience. They hear individual student narratives, collaborate with teachers, and analyze attendance, behavior, and academic data together to track patterns over time.

Using a combination of observation, relational cues, data, and intuition to identify isolation. Here are the **lenses** they rely on.

Developmental Lens: What Should We Expect at This Age?

Every age has expected patterns of:

- peer engagement
- independence
- communication
- emotional regulation
- risk-taking
- identity formation

School counselors look for misaligned developmental behavior:

- **Elementary Example:** A second grader who consistently avoids play is not developmentally typical.
- **Middle School Example:** A seventh grader who has no peer relationships and avoids all group work might be masking social anxiety or rejection sensitivity.

- **High School Example:** A tenth grader who excels academically but has no extracurricular involvement or meaningful peer relationships may be isolated in ways adults miss.

School counselors connect their developmental knowledge to these red flags.

Neuroception Lens: What Does the Student's Nervous System Seem to Be Signaling?

Borrowing from Polyvagal Theory, counselors observe:

SIGNS OF HYPERAROUSAL (FIGHT/FLIGHT):	SIGNS OF HYPOAROUSAL (SHUTDOWN):
✓ irritability ✓ avoidance ✓ perfectionism ✓ rigid posture ✓ startle responses ✓ difficulty staying seated ✓ talking too fast	✓ flat affect ✓ slow responses ✓ withdrawal ✓ fatigue ✓ staring into space ✓ lack of participation

These clues reveal how safe, or unsafe, a student feels internally. School counselors read these cues not as misbehavior, but as **survival strategies**.

Attachment Lens: How Does the Student Seek (or Avoid) Connection?

Attachment styles shape behavior:

AVOIDANT STUDENTS	ANXIOUS STUDENTS	DISORGANIZED STUDENTS
✓ seem independent ✓ resist help ✓ avoid vulnerability ✓ downplay needs	✓ seek reassurance ✓ worry about friendships ✓ read negativity into neutral cues	✓ show inconsistent behavior ✓ fluctuate between clinging and withdrawing

School counselors understand how attachment patterns influence peer relationships.

For example:

- A student who avoids group work isn't necessarily *oppositional*; sometimes, they are protecting themselves from humiliation or rejection.
- A student who laughs nervously when corrected isn't always being *disrespectful*; they are possibly attempting to disarm discomfort.
- A student who withdraws during class discussion may not be *unprepared*; they may be dysregulated or overwhelmed.

School counselors can help ascertain and identify **the "why" behind the behavior**. Then, in collaboration with school social workers and other school services personnel, counselors assist educators with understanding home dynamics, chronic stressors, cultural contexts, and social histories that influence a student's sense of belonging.

They may know:

- the family recently moved
- a caregiver is ill
- there has been loss or separation
- there has been housing instability
- there are cultural reasons for reserved behavior
- the child has experienced bullying or exclusion

This knowledge shapes compassionate responses that help leaders coordinate relational supports. These systems provide predictable opportunities for students to feel seen, supported, and connected, especially during vulnerable moments such as school transitions, schedule changes, or returns after absence.

Beyond individual counseling or advising, school counselors also support the design and implementation of structures that help the entire school align practices around relational safety at scale:

- peer mentoring programs
- skill-building sessions
- small-group counseling
- transition supports
- staff professional development
- schoolwide belonging initiatives
- intervention team collaboration

Let's consider how this might play out for an individual student by reading about Devon.

STUDENT STORY

Devon - Isolation Hiding Behind Anger

Devon arrived in sixth grade with a record of "behavioral issues." Teachers saw explosive outbursts, heard a disrespectful tone, tracked inconsistent homework, and reported frequent office referrals.

But when the school counselor met with him, a different story emerged. Devon had transferred schools multiple times due to family instability. He never had time to settle. He had no consistent peer relationships. Lunchtime was unbearably lonely—he spent it eating quickly and silently and then wandered the courtyard. Devon's nervous system had learned to operate in survival mode. His anger was not defiance; it was **the physiology of loneliness**, activated through fight responses.

The counselor created a plan of support grounded in connection:

- morning check-ins
- a small lunch group
- a predictable adult anchor
- a safe break space when overwhelmed
- gentle, steady presence rather than reactive discipline

Within weeks, Devon's outbursts decreased. Within months, they nearly disappeared.

His story illustrates a vital truth: *Loneliness can look like aggression, avoidance, perfectionism, or withdrawal.* School counselors can use their unique perspective to see beneath the surface and support early interventions that lead to student success.

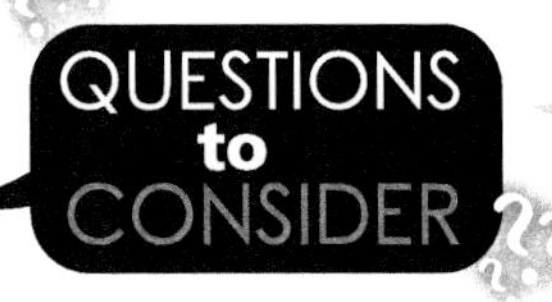

1. What messages do leaders' behaviors send about safety, patience, and support under stress?

2. Do walkthroughs and observations communicate that relationships matter as much as instruction?

3. How are student voices informing your understanding of connection, isolation, and peer dynamics?

4. If adult belonging were treated as a Tier 1 system, what would it look like in daily practice?

5. Where might adult isolation be hidden behind independence, professionalism, or compliance?

- **Leadership attention shapes culture.** When belonging is named and prioritized, teams shift from judgment to shared responsibility.

- **Leaders set the nervous system tone of the building.** Calm, present leadership supports regulation, while reactivity can sustain stress.

- **Visibility is intervention.** Greeting, noticing, and acknowledging students and adults creates powerful regulatory cues.

- **Intentional systems for adult connection** make isolation detectable and support proactive, sustainable regulation.

- **Small, consistent rituals** such as visibility, follow-up, and shared language strengthen adult belonging without requiring large initiatives.

- **Context changes interpretation.** Understanding the story behind behavior shifts responses from reactive discipline to coordinated support.

- **Predictable relational systems** help students navigate transitions, schedule changes, and absences—times when isolation often increases.

Assess connectedness by asking yourself:

- Which student surprised me today?
- Which student seemed withdrawn?
- Which student lit up?
- Who asked for help—verbally or through behavior?
- Which teacher expressed concern about a student's belonging?
- Who needs a check-in tomorrow?

This kind of reflection guides intentional action.

The "One More Question" Check-In

When a student stops by quickly, ask, **"Before you go—how's your heart today?"** It often reveals more than expected.

The "Silent Seat" Technique

Sit near a dysregulated student without demanding conversation. Your presence alone regulates.

The "Name-Remember-Return" Strategy

Choose a student from today's interactions. Remember one detail. Return to it tomorrow.

- "How did the game go?"
- "Did you finish that art project?"
- "How's your sister doing?"

Questions like these build trust quickly.

Belonging isn't a program; it is a practice. School leaders, school staff, and school counselors make this practice sustainable.

The work of connectedness is deeply relational, neurologically informed, and profoundly impactful. With intention and practice, all educators can create moments of safety and connection that prepare students' brains for engagement and transform their school experiences.

However, even with the best intentions and the strongest systems for neural safety, rupture will happen. Disconnection will occur. It's inevitable in the way that humans make mistakes—especially as they are developing and growing. **Chapter 6** discusses what can be done in moments of rupture to repair the connection and rebuild the relationship with accountability and humility.

Repairing and Rebuilding Disconnection

No matter how strong its culture, no matter how well-designed its systems of belonging, and no matter how well-connected the adults in the building seem to be, every school will experience moments of disconnection. Students will feel rejected. Adults will become overwhelmed. Words will be spoken in frustration. Consequences will land harder than intended. Students will experience punishment without understanding. Teachers will feel personally challenged. Administrators will make decisions that inadvertently rupture connection. And sometimes, the harm will be older, brought into the school through years of exclusion, trauma, or inconsistent caregiving.

Disconnection is not a sign that something is wrong with the school. Disconnection is a sign that the school is full of humans.

What differentiates schools that heal from those that accumulate emotional scar tissue is whether they view relational rupture as a personal failure **or** as an opportunity for nervous system repair, identity reorganization, and restored belonging.

The task of this chapter is to explore how schools can become places where students do not collapse beneath conflict, but are **met in it**, held through it, and returned to community stronger than they were before.

Rupture and Repair

There is a phrase in attachment theory that should be on the wall of every school leader's office: "Secure relationships are built not through perfection, but through the cycle of rupture and repair." Children do not grow when relationships never fracture. They grow when fractures **can be repaired.**

A student who has never experienced rupture-resolution in a safe setting learns one of two dangerous beliefs: "Relationship requires perfection," or "Conflict means abandonment."

Both of these beliefs sabotage future relationships, self-regulation, and classroom engagement.

Healthy school communities teach an alternative belief:

We can struggle and still stay connected.

This is not only emotional learning; it is neurological reframing. Each successful repair strengthens the neural circuitry responsible for:

- distress tolerance
- emotional flexibility
- impulse control
- relational trust
- resilience
- conflict recovery

Children who experience repair learn, "My nervous system can survive disconnection and return to safety." Children who do not experience repair often learn "The safest thing is never to risk connection again."

When a student experiences relational rupture, whether through discipline, embarrassment, public correction, peer rejection, or harsh tone, the amygdala interprets the moment as danger. When the brain's survival circuits activate:

- heart rate increases
- breathing changes
- cortisol rises
- hypervigilance spikes
- verbal reasoning decreases
- reflective thinking shuts down

A dysregulated student cannot:

- take responsibility,
- explain what they were thinking,
- calm down and talk it through,

until their nervous system has reestablished basic safety.

This explains why traditional disciplinary sequences fail:

Teacher: *"Tell me why you did that."*
Student: *"I don't know."*
Teacher: *"You need to take responsibility!"*
Student: *"I'm trying!"*

We often interpret this as disrespect. In truth, the student is physiologically incapable of reasoning yet. At that moment, the brain needs co-regulation, emotional safety, and a regulated adult nervous system, not a lecture.

When schools lead with punishment before reestablishing psychological safety, students learn to:

- mask
- appease
- shut down
- intensify fight/flight defenses

Schools that reverse the sequence—**safety first, accountability second**, teach students to:

- reflect without shame
- communicate needs
- consider impact
- participate in problem-solving
- stay connected through conflict

A simple guiding rule for psychological safety: *If the student cannot access their prefrontal cortex, they cannot access responsibility*. Calm the nervous system, then address behavior. In that order.

Lydia's Return to School

Lydia, a tenth grader, was suspended after a heated confrontation with a teacher who interpreted her tone as defiant. In truth, Lydia's anger was masking panic. She had recently moved schools and felt academically insecure. When a classroom assignment triggered feelings of inadequacy, her survival system activated, and a fight response erupted.

When Lydia returned from suspension, the school counselor facilitated a restorative meeting. The teacher opened with a simple, powerful statement, "You still belong here."

Lydia later said, "It was the first time I realized I could start again." At that moment, Lydia's nervous system dropped out of defense mode. Safety cues reactivated the prefrontal cortex. Emotional re-regulation became possible. Learning pathways reopened.

In that single sentence, "You still belong here," the school delivered an essential developmental message: *"Mistakes are events, not identities."* That message changes lives.

The Adult as a Borrowed Nervous System

When students are dysregulated, they need to **borrow the adult's regulation** before they can access their own.

CO-REGULATION IS NOT	CO-REGULATION IS
✗ talking students out of feelings	✓ regulated presence
✗ reasoning with them	✓ steady tone
✗ telling them to calm down	✓ calm breathing
✗ demanding apologies	✓ non-threatening posture
	✓ patient silence
	✓ attuned waiting

There is a neuroscience truth educators need to hear and understand: *A student cannot become regulated if the adult is dysregulated.*

A dysregulated student is essentially asking, "Is it safe enough for me to come out of survival mode?" Educators must understand and engage the shift from "How do I get this student under control?" to "How can I become a regulating force in the room?"

Once the adult's nervous system settles, the student becomes capable of repair.

This is not about being perfect; it is about being **aware**.

One principal taught staff this mantra: "If the student is drowning, we cannot jump in without a life vest." Sometimes the "life vest" is:

- taking five seconds to breathe
- pausing before speaking
- stepping out and tag-teaming with another adult
- lowering volume to reduce threat perception

A regulated adult can de-escalate a conflict in under 60 seconds.

A dysregulated adult can escalate a conflict for the rest of the semester.

Belonging Scripts: Language That Lowers Defenses

Many educators ask, "But what do I say?" Below are language patterns that communicate safety to the nervous system during difficult moments. These sentences:

- reduce shame
- preserve student dignity
- reestablish relationship
- reopen cognitive functioning
- shift the nervous system from defensive to present

1. **Safety and Belonging**

    "You matter here, regardless of what happened."

    "I'm not going anywhere."

    "We're going to get through this together."

2. **Regulation Before Problem-Solving**

    "Right now, I just want to help your body calm down."

    "Take time to breathe through this, no rush."

    "We can talk after your nervous system catches up."

3. **Connection Before Correction**

    "How you're feeling makes sense."

    "It seems like this was a lot for your system."

    "Let's start with what happened. We'll figure out the rest together."

4. **Differentiating Behavior from Identity**

    "This moment doesn't define you."

    "You are not your worst mistake."

    "We can start again."

5. **Reentry Statements**

    "You are welcome back."

    "Let's talk about how to reconnect."

    "You belong even when things go wrong."

These sentences are not signs of weakness. They are **scientifically accurate emotional interventions.**

Students cannot learn accountability while drowning in dysregulation, but once co-regulation reopens the frontal lobes, their brains become ready to process once again.

Many educators assume students inherently know how to:

- apologize
- explain their perspective
- express upset safely
- listen to impact
- restore trust
- rejoin the group

But students come from inconsistent adult responses in:

- homes where rupture never leads to repair
- peer environments that reinforce withdrawal or aggression
- schools where punishment usurped restoration

A student cannot perform reconciliation skills that they have never been taught. Schools must normalize:

- modeling emotional articulation
- teaching restorative language
- rehearsing scripts
- breaking repair into steps
- offering repeated opportunities to try again

Repair becomes a skill to be learned together, not an act of maturity that students must discover alone.

CASE STUDY 1

The Student Who Stopped Trying

Marcus, a quiet and academically capable seventh grader, suddenly stopped completing assignments. His teachers responded the way many do:

- reminders
- redirections
- accountability conversations
- missing assignment notices

Nothing changed. His posture remained flat, eyes down, answers clipped.

What adults did not yet know was that Marcus had recently experienced the death of a grandparent who had lived in the home with him. His grief was unspoken, but visible through his behavior.

The turning point came when one day the school counselor sat beside him and simply said:

"I've noticed your spark has been dimmer lately. When someone's light fades, it usually means something heavy is happening. I'm here if you want someone to hold it with you."

Marcus didn't speak. But his body softened. And for the first time in weeks, there was eye contact.

Two days later, he walked quietly into the counselor's office and said, "I'm tired of pretending I'm okay."

At that moment, repair began. The initial repair was not, at first, a repair of the behavior itself, but rather of **the emotional rupture beneath it all**.

The Outcomes:

- Marcus received space to grieve.
- Teachers adjusted expectations temporarily.
- He slowly re-engaged academically.

His grades improved only after his nervous system experienced being seen.

This is why connection is intervention. Achievement is the by-product.

Group Counseling as the "Neural Gym"

Dr. Stephen Porges, through Polyvagal Theory, describes social engagement as a set of **trainable neural exercises**. Students who participate in small-group counseling gain opportunities to:

- practice reading facial cues
- experience empathy in real time
- experiment with new behaviors in a low-risk space
- receive immediate relational feedback
- regain trust in peer interaction

Group counseling is not about "talking it out." It is about **training the social engagement system**, just as physical therapy trains a muscle. A student who repeats social interactions in a safe environment learns, "Connection does not hurt. Conflict does not destroy. I can recover." In this way, group counseling becomes:

- the rehearsal room for future relational success
- the simulator that prepares students for real-world conflict
- the laboratory where the nervous system learns that safety is possible

The Real Reason Punishment Alone Doesn't Change Behavior

Punitive systems are built on behavioral conditioning: "Bad action + painful consequence = future avoidance." But research consistently shows that punishment decreases behavior **only temporarily**, only when the adult who administers it is present, and only when the student is not in survival mode.

Why? Because punishment often drives **compliance without capacity.** Students may:

- avoid adults,
- shut down emotionally,
- withdraw,
- mask their behavior,
- learn not to get caught,

but they have not learned:

- how to regulate,
- how to repair,
- how to name feelings,
- how to tolerate distress,
- how to resolve conflict,
- or how to reenter community.

Punishment might control the moment. It rarely transforms the future.

What Actually Changes Behavior?

Behavior changes when:

- the nervous system is regulated
- the relationship is preserved
- reflection happens without shame
- the student feels empowered to reenter community
- and the skill that was missing is explicitly taught

The formula is simple:

$$\text{Safety} + \text{Skills} + \text{Support} = \text{Growth.}$$

Punitive consequences alone offer none of these.

The Restorative Approach to Repair

"Restorative practices" have become a buzzword, but many schools miss the core purpose.

Restorative practice does NOT mean:	Authentic restorative work:
• no consequences • everyone just apologizes and moves on • the student has to talk about their feelings on command • forced forgiveness • public confession circles	• repairs harm • restores relationship • teaches future skills • protects dignity • reestablishes belonging

Students should leave restorative conversations not just having survived conflict but having **learned a new way to engage relationally.**

What Makes a Restorative Conversation Effective

Research and field practice show that restorative conversations must include:

1. **Regulated Adults** - If the adult enters dysregulated, the student will mirror it.
2. **Regulated Students** - If the student is in fight/flight or shutdown, reasoning is impossible. Regulation must always come first.
3. **Nonjudgmental Questions** - The purpose is understanding, not interrogation.
4. **Shared Ownership** - This means the student owns their impact, but the adult also reflects on their role (tone, timing, escalation, approach).

5. **A Plan for What Happens Next -** Students need a roadmap for reentry.
6. **A Return to Belonging -** No student should ever return to class unsure of whether the relationship is intact.

A 5-Step Restorative Conversation Framework

Educators often ask, "What do I actually say?"

Below is a reliable 5-step structure.

STEP 1: Regulate

Adult models calm first.

> *"Before we talk, let's just take a moment to slow our breathing."*
> *"Let's take this one step at a time."*
> *"I'm here. We've got time."*

Goal: Lower physiological arousal so reflection becomes possible.

STEP 2: Connect Before Correct

Acknowledge the human experience first.

> *"That seemed like a really intense moment."*
> *"Your feelings about that situation make sense."*
> *"Thank you for staying here and being willing to talk."*

This signals, "You are safe enough to tell the truth."

STEP 3: Story Without Judgment

Invite perspective without blame. Questions like:

> *"What was happening right before the incident?"*
> *"What were you needing in that moment?"*
> *"What did your body feel like when things escalated?"*

These are **nervous system questions**, not moral ones.

STEP 4: Impact + Responsibility

When students are calm, they can finally access empathy and accountability.

> *"Here's how your behavior affected the classroom…"*
>
> *"What do you understand now that you couldn't in the moment?"*
>
> *"What do you think you could do differently next time?"*

Ownership should never come from fear; it should come from understanding.

STEP 5: Reentry Plan

The final step restores dignity, makes logistics clear, and closes the loop.

Examples:

> *"When you walk back in, I'll greet you at the door so you're not walking in alone."*
>
> *"What support do you need from me to succeed?"*
>
> *"Let's plan one sentence you can say if the situation happens again."*

Without reentry, restorative work is incomplete. Schools often struggle with what to do **after** a suspension, removal, meltdown, or major conflict. Students frequently walk back in:

- embarrassed
- unsure of their standing
- disconnected
- silently anxious
- guarded
- feeling the need to mask or defend

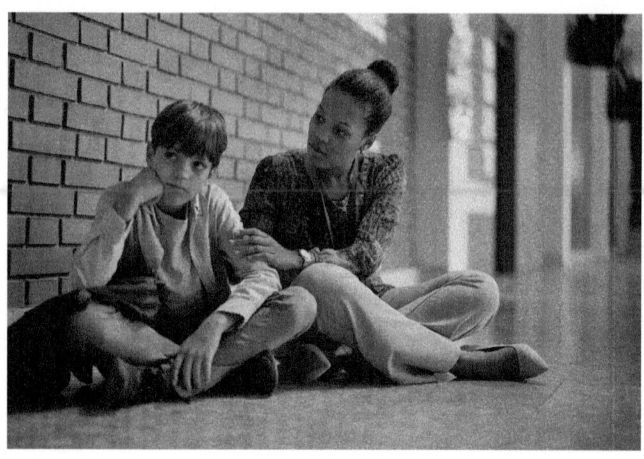

Modeling Humility

One of the most transformative aspects of relational repair happens when **adults model humility**. Not every conflict is caused by student behavior alone. Sometimes adults:

- speak with a sharper tone than intended
- enforce rules inconsistently
- respond out of stress instead of presence
- miss the early signs of dysregulation
- interpret behavior through a biased lens
- escalate instead of de-escalating

When adults own their part, a powerful thing happens. Students learn, "Authority can be honest and still remain strong." This builds respect. Not the compliance kind, but the earned kind.

Sample adult language:

"I was more frustrated than I meant to be, and I'm sorry for the tone I used."

"I realize I didn't give you space to regulate first."

"I see now that my timing made it harder for you to succeed."

"Next time, I'll approach you differently."

Students who never see adults admit fault learn, "Accountability is something done to students, not something modeled for them."

But when educators demonstrate shared responsibility, students learn, "Accountability is something humans do together."

In-the-Moment Scripts for Difficult Situations

Below are scripts educators can use immediately, categorized by escalation scenario.

When the Student is Yelling

"I hear how upset you are. I'm listening."

"You don't have to take this all on yourself. I'll help you."

"Your feelings are allowed. I just want to help your body feel safe."

Why it works: It removes power struggle and signals that the adult will not abandon the student.

When the Student Shuts Down

"You don't have to talk. I'll sit with you, so you don't have to feel alone."

"When you're ready, nod, and we'll take the next step together."

This communicates: "Silence is not rejection. I'm still here."

When the Student Refuses to Follow Directions

Instead of:

"Do it now." or "I said no!"

Try:

"What do you need right now to help you do this?"

"Tell me which step feels hard; I'll help."

This shifts the moment from **power to partnership.**

When the Student is Being Disrespectful

The goal is not to win the ego contest; it's to regulate the nervous system.

> *"I want to understand what's underneath that tone."*

> *"Your words are sharp; your feelings must be intense."*

Students often soften when they realize the adult is attuned rather than threatened.

When the Adult Needs a Pause

Sometimes, regulation needs to happen in the adult first.

> *"I care about handling this well. I'm going to take ten seconds to slow my breathing, and then we'll talk."*

This models regulation as a grown-up skill, not a child demand.

CASE STUDY 2

The Teacher Who Took It Personally

Ms. Whitting, a high-performing teacher, had a ninth-grade student, "Andre," who frequently challenged her instructions and asked "why" in front of the class. Ms. Whitting interpreted this as disrespect and attempted to "command authority," escalating tone and volume.

Andre escalated in response.

When the assistant principal observed the situation, she noticed something different:

- Andre did not escalate with other adults.
- Andre was respectful in one-on-one conversations.
- The conflict emerged only in front of the class.

The assistant principal facilitated a reflective conversation with the teacher: "Help me understand what was happening for you internally in those moments."

Ms. Whitting admitted she felt exposed. She believed the class was watching to see if she "lost control." Andre's questions triggered insecurity, not defiance.

With support, Ms. Whitting reentered the relationship differently. She lowered her volume. She delayed correction until after the lesson. She asked Andre privately, "Do you need clarification, or do you need voice?"

Andre admitted, "Sometimes I don't understand and get embarrassed, so I try to look confident."

They shook hands. A new relationship began.

Andre's behavior improved **without punishment** because the adult shifted from ego to empathy, and the student felt emotionally safe enough to express his real needs.

Human relationships are not built through the absence of rupture. They are built through the **promise of repair.** Every time a student falls apart, loses control, speaks impulsively, makes a poor decision, or pushes relationships away, their nervous system is asking a single question: "Is this a place where I lose belonging when I lose control?"

A belonging-focused school answers, "No! We stay. We repair. We start again."

Students do not become resilient by avoiding conflict. They become resilient by surviving conflict **in the presence of steady, regulated adults.**

Reentry Practices That Work

One of the most healing developmental messages any student can receive is, "You can start again." This sentence communicates that the mistake is over, accountability has been taken, identity is protected, yet belonging remains.

It differentiates "What you did" from "Who you are."

After conflict, the **reentry moment is everything.** Too often, students return to class embarrassed and unsure if they are still welcome. Teachers may also feel tense, resentful, and nervous about another eruption. They often feel alone during student conflict and may worry:

"Am I going to get in trouble with my administration?"

"Does leadership think I can't manage my class?"

"Will this reflect poorly in my evaluation?"

School leaders can change that emotional landscape by communicating:

- **"We are in this together."** – Conflict is a shared responsibility, not a personal failure.
- **"I will support you publicly and coach you privately."** – This protects teacher dignity.
- **"Let's walk through what the student's nervous system experienced."** – This shifts the narrative from "The student was acting out" to "The student was overwhelmed."
- **"What support do YOU need?"** – Many teachers need:
  - debriefing time
  - emotional regulation
  - access to another adult
  - reassurance
  - updated strategies

Teaching is emotional labor; labor that requires replenishment.

What Administrators Should Avoid Saying

The following phrases, even if well-intended, erode trust:

"You just need stronger consequences."

"This shouldn't be happening."

"Classroom management is the issue."

"Why couldn't you stop it before it escalated?"

These statements:

- reinforce educator shame
- activate defensiveness
- discourage teachers from seeking help
- build a culture of fear instead of support

CASE STUDY 3

The Administrator Who Modeled Repair Publicly

At a middle school staff meeting, the principal delivered a stressful blanket-response admonishment regarding a student situation that had occurred earlier that day. His tone came across as sharp and impatient. Teachers left the meeting confused about who was at fault and felt demoralized.

The next morning, the principal addressed the staff:

"I spoke from frustration yesterday instead of presence. My tone didn't model the connection culture we are building, and I'm sorry. I'd like a do-over."

There was a visible shift in the room.

In thirty seconds, the principal demonstrated accountability without defensiveness but with emotional leadership and commitment to shared values. The principal also modeled the very relational repair expected of teachers and students.

A trauma-informed school intent on enhancing belongingness never asks, "Whose fault is this?" Instead, it asks, "What do the adults and students need to succeed?"

The "90-Second Reentry Conversation"

This is the teacher's opportunity to restore the connection between themselves and the student and the student to the classroom. The entire process can happen in **under two minutes**, yet it changes the trajectory of the rest of the day.

1. **Acknowledge the Return** - "I'm glad you're back."
2. **Protect the Relationship** - "We can move forward together."
3. **Name the Skill** - "Today was tough. What will you try next time you feel overwhelmed?"
4. **Offer Partnership** - "If it starts to feel too big again, what signal can you give me?"
5. **Confirm Belonging** - "You still belong in this classroom."

At some point in the repair process, students should be asked two questions:

1. "What do you want me to understand about you?"
2. "What would help you better in moments like this?"

These questions often yield jaw-dropping insights:

"I panic when I think I'm going to disappoint someone."

"I shut down when people raise their voices."

"Being called out in front of the class is hard for me."

"I need a second to think before answering."

The student is not the problem; the unmet need is.

What If the Student Refuses Repair?

Some students decline to engage in:

- restorative practices
- reentry conversations
- apologies
- reflection
- ownership

This is not defiance; it is protection. Students who refuse repair are often communicating:

- *"Attempts to repair have hurt me before."*
- *"Apologies were used as punishment."*
- *"Talking about feelings has been unsafe."*
- *"You haven't proven I can trust this space yet."*
- *"If I open up, I might lose control."*

In these moments, the adult must hold the stance, "I am more patient than your fear."

Possible responses:

- *"We don't have to do this today. I'll be here again tomorrow."*
- *"I won't force you to talk. I just want you to know you're still welcome."*
- *"There are many ways to repair. We can find one that fits you."*

Three truths about student refusal:

- **They are not rejecting the adult; they are protecting themselves.**
- **Time is an intervention.**
- **Consistency is louder than intensity.**

If the adult continues to show up in steady, nonjudgmental, reliable ways, repair will eventually happen.

The Tap-Out: When the Relationship Is Deeply Ruptured

Sometimes the conflict is not momentary; it is cumulative:

- repeated power struggles
- months of misunderstanding
- identity-based wounds
- chronic mutual frustration
- trauma that predates the relationship entirely

In these cases, a third party may need to step in as:

- mediator
- co-regulator
- emotional translator

This is not a failure; it is mature practice. Through the process of mediation, the student and teacher rebuild trust, and something miraculous happens:

The student learns that even painful relationships can heal.

The teacher learns that even the hardest student can return.

The school culture learns "We don't give up on people."

When students repeatedly experience restoration, reentry, and belonging, something profound shifts inside them.

They learn:

- Conflict is survivable.
- Mistakes do not end a relationship.
- Emotional upset is not moral failure.
- Resolution can feel good.
- Trying again is safe.

Neurologically, this builds:

- stronger prefrontal-amygdala connections
- increased emotional resilience
- improved distress tolerance
- more flexible thinking
- enhanced perspective-taking
- vulnerable communication skills

A student raised in a repair-rich environment enters adulthood with:

- better relationship skills
- healthier workplace interactions
- decreased divorce risk
- increased empathy
- better leadership capacity

This is not behavior management; this is **life-readiness preparation.**

1. When rupture occurs, do we prioritize safety and regulation or compliance and control?

2. How explicitly do we teach and model repair skills (e.g., acknowledging harm, making amends, re-entering community)?

3. What language and routines can we normalize to reinforce belonging during and after conflict?

4. Which student behaviors are being managed or suppressed but not truly changed?

5. Are restorative practices embedded daily, or used only as reactive interventions?

6. Do staff feel equipped to co-regulate before correcting? If not, what supports or training are needed?

7. What systems are in place for staff to regulate, reflect, and debrief before re-engaging students?

8. When and how do we involve mediators or co-regulators in more complex or deeply ruptured situations?

9. How do we ensure reentry plans protect dignity and reinforce that mistakes do not define identity?

- **Repair is foundational to learning and belonging.** Without repair, students internalize the harmful beliefs that relationships require perfection or that conflict leads to abandonment. These beliefs undermine regulation, engagement, and trust.

- **Safety must come before correction.** Punitive responses that prioritize compliance over connection often lead to masking, shutdown, or escalation rather than meaningful behavior change.

- **Adults set the regulatory tone.** Shifting from "How do I gain control?" to "How do I become a regulating force?" changes outcomes for both students and staff.

- **Repair is a taught skill**, not an assumed one. Students need explicit instruction and practice in apologizing, understanding the impact, and successfully re-entering the community.

- **Accountability grows through insight, not shame.** True responsibility develops when students understand the impact of their actions within relationships.

- **Reentry restores dignity and belonging.** Effective repair includes clear, supportive pathways for students to return to the community without identity-based labeling.

- **Conflict is relational, not individual.** Repair is a shared process; adults must reflect on their own role and support one another in co-regulation and restoration.

- **Consistent repair builds long-term resilience.** Repeated, supported experiences of rupture and repair strengthen emotional regulation, perspective-taking, and relational competence over time.

RESET, REPAIR, REFLECT

2-Minute Personal Reset

Before students arrive for the day, ask each staff member to briefly reflect:

- When conflict happens, do I tend to move toward control first, or regulation?
- What does my tone, body language, and pace communicate in those moments?

Rally around an anchor phrase: "Connection before correction."

1-Minute Plan for Reentry

Today, when conflict occurs, ensure every student has a clear, dignified return:

- Reinforce: "You still belong here."
- What's the next right thing for you to do?

Avoid: Forced apologies, public correction, or vague expectations.

5-Minute Staff Debrief

At the end of the day or in PLCs, reflect as a staff:

- Where did we **prioritize regulation over control** today?
- Where did we revert to compliance?
- What language or routines worked to support repair?
- When did we need additional support (co-regulator, mediator)?

RUPTURE & REPAIR SCHOOL STAFF REFLECTIONS
Self-Awareness Prompts

Which student behaviors feel personally threatening, and why?

____

____

What is happening inside your own nervous system?

____

____

How did adults handle rupture and repair when you were a child?

____

____

Do you need support before you can give support?

____

____

- -

RUPTURE & REPAIR SCHOOL STAFF REFLECTIONS
Self-Awareness Prompts

Which student behaviors feel personally threatening, and why?

____

____

What is happening inside your own nervous system?

____

____

How did adults handle rupture and repair when you were a child?

____

____

Do you need support before you can give support?

____

____

RUPTURE & REPAIR SCHOOL STAFF REFLECTIONS
Instructional Prompts

What sentence could you start using with students tomorrow that communicates: "You still belong here"?

____

____

In what way can you check in with a student privately after conflict?

____

____

Which skill (emotional, cognitive, relational) was the student lacking in the moment, not just what rule was broken?

____

____

RUPTURE & REPAIR SCHOOL STAFF REFLECTIONS
Instructional Prompts

What sentence could you start using with students tomorrow that communicates: "You still belong here"?

____

____

In what way can you check in with a student privately after conflict?

____

____

Which skill (emotional, cognitive, relational) was the student lacking in the moment, not just what rule was broken?

____

____

RUPTURE & REPAIR SCHOOL STAFF REFLECTIONS
Community Prompts

How can your school shift from "Who caused this?" to "What does this student need?"

____

____

Which students need a fresh start this week?

____

____

How can staff hold each other accountable without blame?

____

____

RUPTURE & REPAIR SCHOOL STAFF REFLECTIONS
Community Prompts

How can your school shift from "Who caused this?" to "What does this student need?"

____

____

Which students need a fresh start this week?

____

____

How can staff hold each other accountable without blame?

____

____

RUPTURE & REPAIR SCHOOL STAFF REFLECTIONS
Administrator Prompts

How do I support teachers without assuming they failed? ___________________________

____

When teachers struggle, do they feel safe coming to school leadership? ______________

____

Does our school react to student behavior, or strive to understand it? ________________

____

Where are punitive measures replacing skill-building supports? _____________________

____

What systems are in place for reentry after removal or suspension?__________________

____

How often do school leaders model repair publicly? ______________________________

____

RUPTURE & REPAIR SCHOOL STAFF REFLECTIONS
Administrator Prompts

How do I support teachers without assuming they failed? ___________________________

____

When teachers struggle, do they feel safe coming to school leadership? ______________

____

Does our school react to student behavior, or strive to understand it? ________________

____

Where are punitive measures replacing skill-building supports? _____________________

____

What systems are in place for reentry after removal or suspension?__________________

____

How often do school leaders model repair publicly? ______________________________

____

Repair reestablishes connection - safety - belonging

Neurologically, this means the brain can return to learning. No academic intervention can out-compete a dysregulated nervous system. Connection, therefore, is not a luxury. It is **instructional infrastructure.**

When repair becomes normalized, teachers take misbehavior less personally, and students experience accountability without humiliation. We move from: "You messed up" to "This moment is part of who you're becoming."

And students step into adulthood knowing something many adults never learn: "I do not have to be perfect to be worthy of belonging."

Envisioning Future-Ready Graduates

Future-ready schools understand that the most enduring outcomes of education are not only academic but also relational. The modern workforce consistently names communication, collaboration, emotional regulation, adaptability, and conflict navigation as essential competencies. These skills are not learned through lectures or compliance systems. They are learned through repeated relational experiences where students practice staying connected under pressure.

A future-ready school does not ask, "Are students comfortable?" It asks, "Are students learning how to stay human, connected, and accountable in moments of discomfort?" That is workforce readiness. That is life readiness.

From Classroom Practice to Adult Competence

The future our students are entering will demand far more than content mastery. Adults are increasingly required to:

- collaborate across differences
- tolerate feedback
- repair after conflict
- regulate under pressure
- remain engaged when things go wrong

Students do not learn these competencies in isolation, nor do they acquire them through compliance-based systems. Instead, students develop them through repeated relational experiences in environments where accountability and connection coexist.

Students do not magically acquire relational skills at graduation. They develop them, or fail to, through thousands of daily interactions with peers and adults.

Future-ready schools make the transfer explicit: *what we practice here is what you will use out there.*

STUDENT STORY

The Missed Deadline

Mason, a high school senior, is really feeling the crunch of the final term looming ahead of him. With a new soccer season, orchestra requirements, and a part-time job, he's starting to feel overwhelmed and, jarringly, realizes he missed a major deadline.

In desperation, he makes an appointment with his teacher, Mr. Dodd, expecting a punitive consequence. Instead, the teacher begins with curiosity:

"Help me understand what happened."

Mason admits feeling overwhelmed and avoiding the assignment.

Leaning on restorative conversation techniques, Mr. Dodd helps Mason name the impact of the missing assignment, develop a recovery plan, and rehearse how to communicate proactively next time.

This moment teaches more than responsibility. It teaches:

- how to own mistakes without collapsing into shame
- how to repair trust after failure
- how to problem-solve collaboratively
- how to remain connected while being held accountable

These are adult skills.

When schools consistently respond this way, students internalize a critical belief: *Mistakes are survivable, and relationships can hold accountability.* This belief directly transfers to adult environments such as workplaces, families, and communities where rupture is inevitable and repair determines success.

Future-ready education requires schools to stop assuming students "will figure it out later." Instead, schools must build "later" into "now." Every restorative conversation, reentry practice, and co-regulation moment is a rehearsal for adult life. When schools intentionally teach these skills, graduates leave not just with knowledge, but with the capacity to function in complex human systems.

The Future Cost of NOT Teaching Relational Readiness

Schools track academic readiness meticulously, yet rarely assess relational readiness—the ability to engage, repair, regulate, and collaborate under stress.

Future-ready schools recognize that relational readiness is as essential as literacy or numeracy.

When schools avoid relational work, students still learn, but often the wrong lessons. They learn avoidance, compliance, masking, or aggression. These strategies may preserve short-term order, but they undermine long-term functioning.

STUDENT STORY

The First Job Exit Interview

Shanna came home after quitting her first job. "I guess I just didn't know how to talk to my supervisor," she admitted later. Feedback felt like rejection. Conflict felt unsafe. She ended up leaving the job feeling insecure and struggling to understand what happened.

Contrast this with Inta, who started her first job after high school. Her supervisor noticed something almost immediately. It wasn't that Inta knew more or worked harder. It was how she handled moments that usually derailed new employees.

In her third week, she was assigned a project with unclear expectations and a tight deadline. Instead of guessing or going silent, Inta asked, "I want to make sure I'm aiming at the right target. Can you clarify what success looks like here?" The conversation stayed calm. The work stayed on track.

Later, during a team review, she received some direct feedback on the project. She listened, paused, and replied, "That makes sense. Can you help me understand where I should adjust?" No defensiveness. No shutdown. Just steady engagement.

When a miscommunication with a coworker created tension, Inta addressed it directly but respectfully. "I think we missed each other earlier," she said. "Can we reset?" The issue was resolved quickly. The relationship stayed intact.

None of this was dramatic, and that is the point.

Inta had attended a repair-rich school, one where conflict was expected, feedback was normal, and adults modeled how to stay present when things went wrong. Over time, her nervous system learned that difficulty isn't danger and correction isn't rejection.

Her supervisor quietly noticed the contrast. Other capable new hires avoided clarification, took feedback personally, or withdrew under pressure. The difference wasn't intelligence or motivation. It was relational readiness.

That is what future-ready education looks like in real life.

Relational readiness is built when schools:

- normalize help-seeking
- teach emotional articulation
- rehearse difficult conversations
- model accountability without humiliation
- treat repair as a skill, not a character trait

When students graduate without these experiences, they may appear competent but lack durability. When they graduate with them, they enter adulthood equipped to navigate complexity rather than avoid it.

Future-ready schools begin asking new questions:

- Can our students stay connected when things go wrong?
- Can they repair after rupture?
- Can they regulate under pressure?

These capacities predict long-term success as powerfully as any transcript.

Relational Capacity as a Professional Leadership Skill

Future-ready schools confront this reality honestly: *Academic success without relational capacity is fragile.* The cost shows up later as burnout, disengagement, failed partnerships, and leadership breakdown.

By contrast, schools that systematize belonging graduate students who know how to struggle openly, repair honestly, and remain connected under pressure. These students are not "softer." They are stronger because their nervous systems have practiced recovery.

Belonging practices are not indulgences. They are prevention. They protect students from carrying maladaptive survival strategies into adulthood and replace them with skills that sustain careers, relationships, and well-being.

The future will not be defined solely by information but by interaction. Automation may replace various tasks; it will not replace relationships. Future-ready schools prepare students accordingly.

STUDENT STORY

The Future-Ready Graduate Who Came Back

Years after graduation, Mathew returned to his local high school for an alumni event at a football game. At that event, he was recognized for his exceptional work in the field of AI integration systems.

His speech was well-received, and he graciously accepted the certificate they presented to him, but, through the crowd of hand-shakers and well-wishers, he was looking for one specific person. After scanning the crowd and asking around a bit, he finally found her—former principal Dr. Carter.

As he shook her hand, he said, "You know, I didn't realize it then, but the way all the teachers and staff here handled conflict and approached challenges changed how I handle it now. I don't panic when things go wrong. I know how to talk, fix, and move forward."

In a world where AI technology is rapidly expanding into our workplaces, the ability to connect with people in authentic ways is more invaluable than ever. Thank you for helping me become a better employee and a better person."

This is the long game of education. When students repeatedly experience:

- safety before accountability,
- repair after rupture,
- dignity during discipline,
- and belonging that outlasts mistakes,

they internalize a powerful truth:

I can stay connected to myself and others when things get hard.

That truth becomes identity. And identity shapes destiny.

From Initiative to Identity

Sustaining a school culture built on belonging practices that produce future-ready graduates is not simply about repetition; it is about evolution. Initial initiatives such as morning greetings, welcome circles, or orientation programs serve as catalysts. Identity formation occurs as students repeatedly encounter affirming messages and generalized experiences that are reliably present throughout their educational journeys.

The trajectory can be understood in four phases:

1. **Initiative** – Early inclusion strategies signal that the student matters.
2. **Consistency** – Repetition of affirming practices builds trust and predictability.
3. **Internalization** – Students begin to integrate these experiences into their self-concept.
4. **Identity Formation** – Belonging becomes part of who the student is, not just what the environment offers.

Future-ready schools do not just teach students how to perform. They teach them how to relate. And that may be the most important preparation of all.

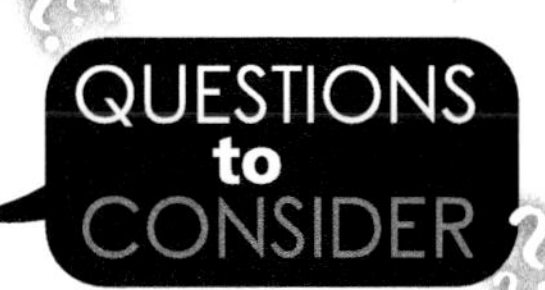

1. How intentionally are we preparing students for a future where human interaction—not just information—defines success?

2. Do our systems ensure that mistakes and conflict become learning opportunities, rather than moments of shame or disconnection?

3. Are we teaching students primarily how to perform, or how to relate, recover, and lead under pressure?

4. How do we know that students can transfer relational skills learned in school to real-world contexts like work, family, and community?

5. Which of our practices are short-term initiatives, and which are consistent enough to shape identity and belonging over time?

- **Relational competence is future readiness.** Communication, collaboration, emotional regulation, adaptability, and conflict navigation are as essential as academic skills—and increasingly define success in a world where automation can replace tasks, but not human connection.

- **The future belongs to those who can relate, not just perform.** Schools must prepare students not only to achieve, but to engage, recover, and lead when challenges, feedback, and conflict arise.

- **Discomfort fluency is a critical skill.** Future-ready environments teach students to remain connected, accountable, and regulated in moments of difficulty—not avoid or escape them.

- **Daily interactions are the training ground.** Every restorative conversation, co-regulation moment, and reentry experience builds the relational habits students will carry into workplaces, families, and communities.

- **Identity is shaped through consistent experience.** Belonging becomes a durable life skill when relational practices move beyond isolated initiatives and become embedded into everyday school culture.

- **Repair, reflection, and re-engagement build lifelong capacity.** Students who repeatedly experience healthy conflict and successful repair develop resilience, perspective-taking, and relational confidence.

- **Future-ready schools graduate relationally competent adults.** Success is measured not just by what students know, but by their ability to struggle openly, repair authentically, and move forward in connection with others.

Conclusion

Across these chapters, one truth has emerged again and again: *students do not struggle because they lack motivation, resilience, or capability. They struggle when their nervous systems are overloaded by isolation or threat.* They **thrive** when the environment reliably answers the brain's most basic questions:

Am I safe here? Do I matter?

Those same questions follow students into adulthood—into workplaces, relationships, communities, and leadership roles.

The work of creating belonging is not dramatic or grand. It happens in seconds. In tone. In posture. In who is noticed and who is missed. In how adults respond when things go wrong. Over time, these moments accumulate into something powerful: *a school culture that regulates rather than reacts, connects rather than controls, and supports students through difficulty instead of withdrawing relationship when it is most needed.* These are the same conditions that prepare students to collaborate, receive feedback, navigate conflict, and remain grounded in high-stakes adult environments.

The neuroscience is clear—when safety is predictable, the brain opens. When acceptance is unconditional, identity stabilizes. When connection is intentionally cultivated, isolation loses its grip. These are not sentimental ideals; they are neurological necessities. They shape cortisol levels, executive function, attention, memory, and motivation. They determine whether students engage or retreat, speak up or shut down, persist or disengage—patterns that follow them far beyond graduation.

What changes school cultures is not a single strategy, but consistency across people and places. When every adult in the school building shares a common language of safety, acceptance, friendship, and repair, belonging stops being dependent on luck. It becomes infrastructure. Students no longer have to wonder if someone will notice their absence, their effort, or their distress. They learn, implicitly and repeatedly, how healthy systems respond when humans struggle.

Equally important, this work transforms adults. When educators regulate first, when they replace shaming punishment with restorative repair, and when they protect connection rather than postpone it, burnout softens. Educating becomes more sustainable, more human, and more aligned with the long arc of development—not just in terms of academic outcomes but also in terms of life readiness.

When schools commit to this way of operating, the outcomes speak for themselves. Not because students suddenly change, but because the environment does. And when belonging becomes the system, connectedness becomes a lived experience, a core aspect of student identity, and a transferable life skill. That skill prepares young people not just to succeed in school, but to thrive in the complex, relational world they are entering.

Tools for the Toolkit

Minute Meetings

These are short, one-on-one check-ins with every student that help you uncover patterns that may otherwise be difficult to notice. These "Minute Meetings" with students are extremely efficient diagnostics that you can easily adapt to fit the needs of the school community. Use pen and paper, a spreadsheet, or an online form—whatever works best for your capabilities and access.

Questions include:

- "How's your school year going?"
- "Do you feel connected to peers?"
- "Who do you talk to when you need help?"
- "What part of the day feels hardest?"

Minute Meetings often reveal:

- students with zero trusted adults
- students being quietly bullied
- students masking anxiety with compliance
- students experiencing external stressors

Minute Meetings (Example)

Student Name	Q1 How's your school year going? (Likert Scale)	Q2 Do you feel connected to peers?	Q3 Who do you talk to when you need help?	Q4 What part of the day feels hardest?	Notes:	Follow-Up:
Amy Moore	3	No	Dr. Jones	Math	Wants help with social activity at lunch	Add to Lunch Bunch group
Student 2						
Student 3						

Minute Meetings

Student Name	Q1 How's your school year going? (Likert Scale)	Q2 Do you feel connected to peers?	Q3 Who do you talk to when you need help?	Q4 What part of the day feels hardest?	Notes:	Follow-Up:

Classroom Observation Template for Social Patterns

Non-evaluative data that helps teachers adjust routines to support belonging.

Counselors sometimes observe classrooms not to evaluate instruction, but to:

- track who participates
- watch interactions
- identify who is marginalized
- observe seating patterns
- notice body language

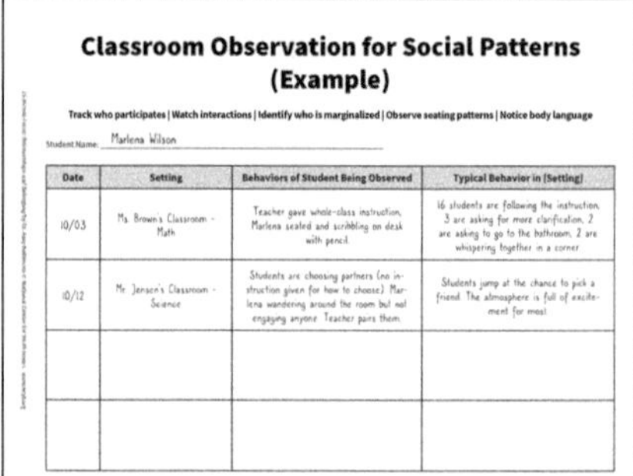

Classroom Observation for Social Patterns (Example)

Track who participates | Watch interactions | Identify who is marginalized | Observe seating patterns | Notice body language

Student Name: Marlena Wilson

Date	Setting	Behaviors of Student Being Observed	Typical Behavior in [Setting]
10/03	Ms. Brown's Classroom - Math	Teacher gave whole-class instruction, Marlena seated and scribbling on desk with pencil.	16 students are following the instruction, 3 are asking for more clarification, 2 are asking to go to the bathroom, 2 are whispering together in a corner
10/12	Mr. Jensen's Classroom - Science	Students are choosing partners (no instruction given for how to choose). Marlena wandering around the room but not engaging anyone. Teacher pairs them.	Students jump at the chance to pick a friend. The atmosphere is full of excitement for most

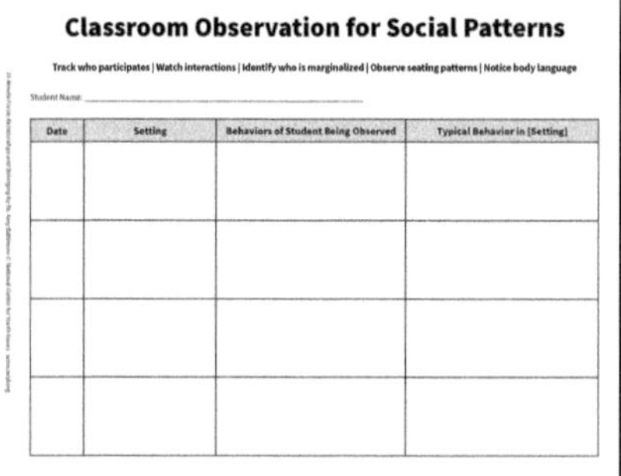

Classroom Observation for Social Patterns

Track who participates | Watch interactions | Identify who is marginalized | Observe seating patterns | Notice body language

Student Name: ________________

Date	Setting	Behaviors of Student Being Observed	Typical Behavior in [Setting]

Internalizing Behavior Screening

The Student Risk Screening Scale, when used ethically and collaboratively, provides invaluable insight.

Screening tools help counselors:

- identify often misunderstood or overlooked behaviors
- examine risk factors
- track emotional health
- monitor progress over time

The screening scale includes seven items measuring externalizing behaviors and five items measuring internalizing behaviors. These include the following:

- steal
- lie, cheat, sneak
- behavior problem
- peer rejection
- low academic achievement
- negative attitude
- aggressive behavior
- emotionally flat
- shy, withdrawn
- sad, depressed
- anxious
- lonely

Teachers rate the students in their class or homeroom based on observation and perceptions only. Rating ranges from 1–5, with 1 being the least extreme behavior and 5 being the most extreme. This is not a diagnostic tool. The data that is discovered from the use of this tool will not be used to label students, but to drive district and school decisions around student supports and services.

Examples can be found at: https://www.ci3t.org/screening.

Transition Checkpoints

Key transition points often reveal isolation. A Transition Checkpoint is a brief, structured check-in built into the school calendar so that no student moves through a major transition unnoticed:

- moving from elementary to middle school
- moving from middle to high school
- transferring to a new school mid-year
- returning after hospitalization or suspension
- re-joining after a lengthy absence

How to use it:

At each identified transition point, a designated adult meets briefly with the student—five to ten minutes is sufficient—using a simple set of questions:

- "How are you feeling about this change?"
- "Is there anyone here you feel connected to?"
- "What feels hardest right now?"
- "What would help you feel more settled?"

Responses are noted and shared with the student support team as needed. The goal is not to assess or diagnose, but to signal to the student that someone is paying attention—and to catch early signs of isolation before they become entrenched.

Who uses it:

School counselors, advisors, homeroom teachers, or any designated relational anchor. In larger schools, this responsibility can be distributed across grade-level teams to ensure coverage.

When to use it:

At each transition point listed above, ideally within the first two weeks of the change. A follow-up check-in two to four weeks later helps confirm whether the student has established connection or needs additional support.

DOWNLOADABLE RESOURCES AND TEMPLATES

Please visit **ncyi.org/downloadable-resources** to access the downloadable resources.

Enter the code below to unlock the resources:

BELONGING616

References

Block, P. (2018). *Community: The structure of belonging*. Berrett-Koehler.

Brown, M. A. (2018). *Creating restorative schools*. Living Justice Press.

Cohen, G. L. (2023). *Belonging: The science of creating connection and bridging divides*. W. W. Norton & Company.

Colombetti, G. (2014). *The feeling body: Affective science meets the enactive mind*. MIT Press.

Covarrubias, R. (2024). What does it mean to belong? An interdisciplinary integration of theory and research on belonging. *Social and Personality Psychology Compass, 18*(1), e12858.

Desautels, L. L. (2024). *Connections over compliance: Rewiring our perceptions of discipline*. Wyatt-MacKenzie Publishing.

Healey, K., & Stroman, C. (2021). Structures for belonging: A synthesis of research on belonging-supportive learning environments. *Student experience research network*.

Margherio, S. M., Evans, S. W., & Owens, J. S. (2019). Universal screening in middle and high schools: Who falls through the cracks? *School Psychology, 34*(6), 591–602. https://doi.org/10.1037/spq0000337.

Mansoor, I. (2025). Exploring the interplay between attachment styles and neuroception: Insights from polyvagal theory. *International Journal of Social Sciences Bulletin, 3*(10), 328–336.

Moore, C. (2014). *The resilience breakthrough*. Greenleaf Book Group Press.

Nicoli, L., & Bolognini, S. (2022). From what to how: A conversation with Stefano Bolognini on emotional attunement. *The Psychoanalytic Quarterly, 91*(3), 443–477. https://doi.org/10.1080/00332828.2022.2118502

Porges, S. W. (2022). Polyvagal theory: A science of safety. *Frontiers in Integrative Neuroscience, 16*, 871227.

Rejaän, Z., van der Valk, I. E., & Branje, S. (2022). The role of sense of belonging and family structure in adolescent adjustment. *Journal of Research on Adolescence, 32*(4), 1354–1368.

Scarson, C. N. (2025). *The Power of Attachment: Healing Trauma with the Body and the Nervous System* (Master's thesis, Pacifica Graduate Institute).

Van der Kolk, B. A. (2014). *The body keeps the score: Brain, mind, and body in the healing of trauma*. Viking.

About the Author

DR. AMY BALTIMORE is a former missionary kid who grew up experiencing first-hand what it is like to serve the needs of children with deep developmental trauma. She began her career by leaning into her passion for supporting the positive growth and development of students through school counseling. As time went on, she realized the adults need just as much support as the students. So, she stepped into the role of serving as a district leader for school counseling…currently with Metro Nashville Public Schools.

Her professional experiences also include serving on the Board of Directors for the Tennessee School Counselor Association, and on advisory councils for the Tennessee Department of Education. She has been an adjunct professor and frequent speaker at various higher ed events and state conferences. She is a Nationally Board Certified Counselor and a certified trainer for Restorative Practices, Building Strong Brains (ACEs/PCEs), The 6 Pillars of Trauma-Informed Schools, and Youth Mental Health First Aid.

Amy is happily married and has two amazing children who have grown and flown. She loves any activity involving sunshine and warm weather. On any given sunny day you can find her at the lake on her paddleboard, or on a bicycle riding the greenway, or hiking with her husband toward one of the many waterfalls found in Middle Tennessee.

Also Available from Amy

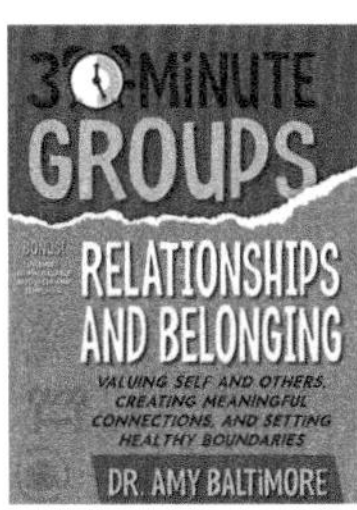

30-Minute Groups: Relationships and Belonging
Valuing Self and Others, Creating Meaningful Connections, and Setting Healthy Boundaries

Topics include social awareness, empathy, communication, and understanding different viewpoints. The lessons and activities in this thoughtfully crafted resource are designed to help students understand their own emotions and perspectives, recognize social cues, and develop the crucial interpersonal skills needed to build and maintain positive, healthy relationships.

A Brief Look at Amy's Speaker Sessions

We're Not All Friends, and That's OK

Creating meaningful connections by understanding how our similarities and differences empower us, and realizing that setting healthy boundaries in relationships promotes mutual respect and understanding, reduces pressure and stress, and increases our confidence and ability to access personal growth.

Relationships and Belonging: Why Students Struggle in Isolation, but Thrive in Connection

Students can often appear socially integrated, but instead they feel unseen or unsafe in the learning environment. In that mindset they struggle, and sometimes, refuse to engage in learning.

This workshop introduces practical ways educators can diagnose disconnection, distinguish healthy solitude from harmful isolation, and build school-wide systems of consistent relational experiences that foster a culture of belonging. Participants leave with simple, actionable strategies to help student brains thrive as they anticipate safety, engage in positive relational connections, and develop a readiness to learn.

Demystifying Advocacy for School Counselors

Your voice matters! As a school counselor you can lean into the ASCA National Model and additional resources to become a strong advocate for each and every student at your local school level, the district level, and even the state level.

Empowering the School Counselor and Administrator Relationship

What do school counselors need to get their programs off the ground – administrators! What do administrators need to fill the gaps for student support – school counselors! The two go hand in hand. Through the strategic use of data to close gaps in student outcomes, collaboration between the school counselor and school administrator yields improved results for student academic achievement, attendance, and social behavior.

The Crisis of Change: From Surviving to Thriving

If there is one constant in education today, it is "change." Change is inevitable and we can't seem to escape it; so how do we lean into it and do more than just survive the onslaught? Here we will lay it all out on the table and openly discuss the crises and conflicts we encounter when change occurs, then we will grapple with some ways to engage with the change and come out the other side thriving in our work as educators.

Motivational Interviewing in Schools: Helping Students Help Themselves

Half of our students don't want us to tell them what to do, and the other half want us to tell them exactly what to do so they don't have to come up with solutions themselves. Motivational Interviewing (MI) offers a practical middle path by empowering students to uncover their own motivations, strengths, and next steps.

In this session, you will learn core MI techniques that foster student ownership, deepen critical thinking, and reduce resistance. Participants will leave with strategies they can immediately integrate into conversations to guide students toward meaningful, self-driven change.

Polish Your Practice: Enhance Solution-Focused Brief Therapy with Integrative Practices for Student Support

Refine and elevate student-support practices by enhancing Solution-Focused Brief Therapy with the integration of complementary therapeutic strategies such as Motivational Interviewing, Cognitive Behavioral Therapy techniques, Person-Centered counseling approaches, and Reality Therapy goal-oriented guidance.

Through interactive exercises and real-world scenarios, you will learn how to integrate these approaches in a seamless, flexible way and explore how each method uniquely empowers students to identify their own resources, envision goals, and take actionable steps toward success. By the end of the workshop, you will leave with a polished set of tools to inspire hope and encourage your students to take ownership of their personal growth.

For more sessions, visit ncyionline.org/speakers

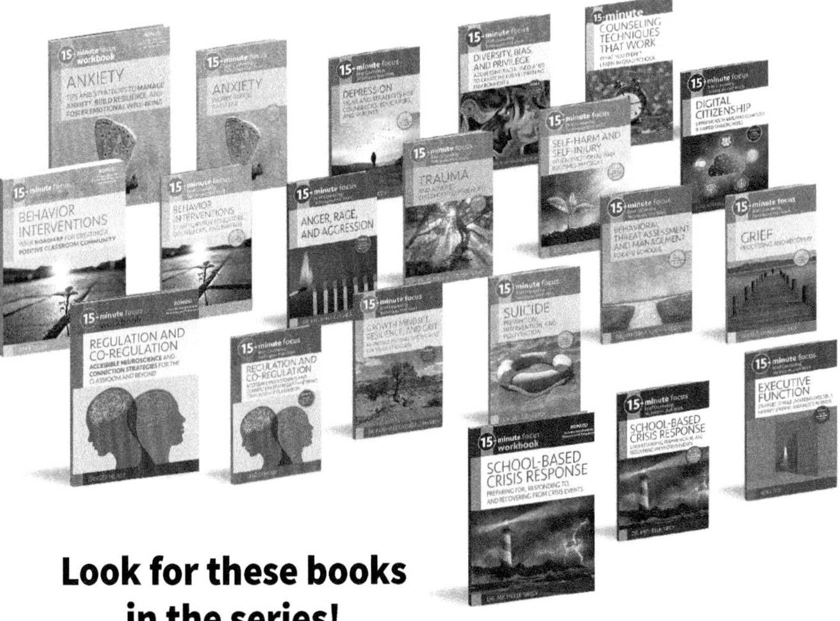

Look for these books in the series!

- 15-Minute Counseling Techniques that Work
- 15-Minute Focus: Anger, Rage, and Aggression
- 15-Minute Focus: Anxiety
- 15-Minute Focus: Anxiety Workbook
- 15-Minute Focus: Behavior Interventions
- 15-Minute Focus: Behavior Interventions Workbook
- 15-Minute Focus: Behavioral Threat Assessment and Management for K-12 Schools
- 15-Minute Focus: Depression
- 15-Minute Focus: Digital Citizenship
- 15-Minute Focus: Diversity, Bias, and Privilege

- 15-Minute Focus: Executive Function
- 15-Minute Focus: Grief
- 15-Minute Focus: Growth Mindset, Resilience, and Grit
- 15-Minute Focus: Regulation and Co-Regulation
- 15-Minute Focus: Regulation and Co-Regulation Workbook
- 15-Minute Focus: School-Based Crisis Response
- 15-Minute Focus: Self-Harm and Self-Injury
- 15-Minute Focus: Suicide
- 15-Minute Focus: Trauma and Adverse Childhood Experiences

About NCYI

National Center for Youth Issues provides educational resources, training, and support programs to foster the healthy social, emotional, and physical development of children and youth. Since our founding in 1981, NCYI has established a reputation as one of the country's leading providers of teaching materials and training for counseling and student-support professionals. NCYI helps meet the immediate needs of students throughout the nation by ensuring those who mentor them are well prepared to respond across the developmental spectrum.

Connect With Us Online!

@nationalcenterforyouthissues

@ncyi

@nationalcenterforyouthissues